EVERYDAY
HEROES

INSPIRATIONAL STORIES FROM MEN AND WOMEN
IN THE CANADIAN ARMED FORCES

EDITED BY
JODY MITIC

PUBLISHED BY SIMON & SCHUSTER
New York   London   Toronto   Sydney   New Delhi

Simon & Schuster Canada
A Division of Simon & Schuster, Inc.
166 King Street East, Suite 300
Toronto, Ontario M5A 1J3

This book was made possible through partnership with The Memory Project Speakers Bureau. Please visit www.thememoryproject.com for more information.

An excerpt of Private Michael Czuboka's story was originally published in the 2008 edition of *The Patrician* magazine. It is reprinted here with permission.

Reasonable efforts have been made to contact copyright holders for permission and to give credit. If additional information is provided, changes may be made to future printings.

This Simon & Schuster Canada edition October 2017

SIMON & SCHUSTER CANADA and colophon are registered trademarks of Simon & Schuster, Inc.

For information about special discounts for bulk purchases, please contact Simon & Schuster Special Sales at 1-800-268-3216 or CustomerService@simonandschuster.ca.

Manufactured in the United States of America

1   3   5   7   9   10   8   6   4   2

Library and Archives Canada Cataloguing in Publication

Mitic, Jody, author
Everyday heroes : inspirational stories from men and women in the Canadian Armed Forces / Jody Mitic.
Issued in print and electronic formats.
ISBN 978-1-5011-6807-9 (softcover).—ISBN 978-1-5011-6808-6 (ebook)
1. Canada—Armed Forces—Biography. 2. Canada. Canadian Armed Forces—Biography. 3. Veterans—Canada—Biography. 4. Soldiers—Canada—Biography. 5. Canada—History, Military—20th century. 6. Canada—History, Military—21st century.
I. Title.
U54.C2M58 2017   355.0092'271   C2017-902102-8
                                           C2017-902103-6

ISBN 978-1-5011-6807-9
ISBN 978-1-5011-6808-6 (ebook)

To the men and women of the Canadian Armed Forces,
past, present, and future, and the public that supports them

CONTENTS

CONTENTS

THE HOME FRONT

PEACEKEEPING

AFGHANISTAN

CONTENTS

EVERYDAY HEROES

INTRODUCTION

Like many young Canadians, I dreamed of joining the military from an early age. As a young recruit, I quickly discovered that the Canadian Armed Forces are full of fierce fighters. The men and women in our ranks are some of the best trained military in the world, and they are also the most generous people I have ever met. I toured in Kosovo and Afghanistan, and I've seen firsthand how wherever we go, our reputation of diplomacy and kindness follows. We bring a human touch to the conflict at hand. And that's often left unsaid.

Now, after two decades serving this country, my greatest mission is to encourage Canadians to get to know the men and women wearing the Canadian flag on their shoulders. This collection of inspiring stories is an invitation to do just that: to see beyond the uniform to the person. Whether it's the young recruit eager to join a world war, the reservist called to respond to a disaster on our own shores, or the medic treating patients for Ebola in Sierra Leone, each one has dedicated him- or herself to protecting our Canadian values at home and abroad. In these pages, you'll read about daring acts of bravery but also the everyday sacrifices and unsung heroism characteristic of the men and women who have answered the call to serve.

Jody Mitic

WORLD
WAR II

Kingston Boy "Safe in Britain," 1945

FLYING OFFICER STUART CRAWFORD (RET)

*We were at 17,500 feet, on track and on time. It would
take fifteen minutes to fly through the defenses of
Hamburg. From my position I could see everything
around me and all hell was breaking loose. There
were many searchlights and anti-aircraft guns, and
I could see puffs of black smoke all around, quite
spectacular, but all was calm in our aircraft.*

I joined the air force when I was twenty, to be a photographer. I'd
been working for the *Whig-Standard* in Kingston as a paper boy, and
the circulation manager there was also a photographer. He taught
me everything I knew, and when he joined the air force photography
department, he said, "We have a great photography department in
Ottawa; why don't you join us?"

When I reported, I was interviewed in Ottawa and was told I qualified for aircrew. I figured, why not take a chance? I didn't want to get
seasick in the navy, and I didn't want to walk, which would have been
the army, so I thought, well, flying might be better. It took two years'
training all over southern Ontario—Belleville, Trenton, Fingal, and
London—and then I continued in Britain.

I ended up as a bomb aimer in the 419 Moose Squadron in 6 Group Bomber Command. We were in a Lancaster with a seven-man crew. Five of us were up front—a wireless operator, a navigator, a flight engineer, the pilot, and me. I sat beside the navigator. We were behind a curtain, so we couldn't see much of anything, but we were quite comfortable—warm really—although crowded. I couldn't complain, though. The poor tail and mid-upper gunners were operating in minus-forty-degree temperatures. It wasn't nice back there!

On the morning of April 8, 1945, we were told we would be flying over Germany that night. The excitement started in the briefing room. It wasn't fear, just extreme tension. Groans, mutterings, and chatter started up. You paid attention to every word that was spoken, particularly those of us who were navigators and bomb aimers because there was a tremendous amount of memory work involved—the tracks we were supposed to take, turning points, latitude and longitude, temperatures, wind and drift, plus much more. And, the target was Hamburg! That was a famous target, one of the heaviest in Europe.

I had a premonition before that particular trip. So much so that I went to see the padre. He asked if I wanted a prayer. "No," I said. "It's going to be an interesting evening, but it's not going to be fatal." That's what I felt. Excitement somehow, and that it was going to be different. I also told the crew and my friend Len.

Every time we went down the runway, the ground crew waved to us and gave us a thumbs-up. With an aircraft like that we had fourteen thousand pounds of dynamite and two thousand gallons of high-test gasoline, and if something went wrong, we were goners. That night, I was looking out the window and guess who I saw at the end of the runway? The padre! I wasn't a particularly religious person, but he was there, and I saw him giving me the thumbs-up.

The flight out was uneventful—if you could call a trip like that uneventful. It was the middle of the night, and there were 440 aircraft going on to the target. None of us had lights on. With 440 aircraft, that's a field about eighteen miles long by five miles wide. So we had to keep a sharp eye out!

Twenty minutes before target, I did my last fix on the Gee radar set, plotted it, then moved from the navigator table to the dark bomb aimer's position in the nose of the Lancaster to set up the bombsight and the many switches on the bomb aimer's panel. We were at 17,500 feet, on track and on time. It would take fifteen minutes to fly through the defenses of Hamburg. From my position I could see everything around me and all hell was breaking loose. There were many search-lights and anti-aircraft guns, and I could see puffs of black smoke all around, quite spectacular, but all was calm in our aircraft. Hugh, the skipper, and myself were the only ones talking.

I could see the fake target ahead to the right and the correct coloured markers dropped by the Pathfinder aircraft ahead on the Blohm & Voss Shipyards.

"*Bomb doors open!*" I called. I began directing Hugh—"left, left, steady"—lining up the coloured flares in the bombsight. Then I pressed the bomb-release button and called out, "Bombs gone!" What a great relief. We dropped down to a lower altitude to avoid night fighters.

The next thing I knew, our starboard engine was on fire! We were able to put it out swiftly, but then I saw a fighter flare at eleven o'clock high. I informed the skipper and moved up to my two guns, but I couldn't use them because they operated off the starboard inner en-gine. That's when things got interesting. The starboard *outer* engine caught on fire, but we managed to put it out.

We began to lose altitude quickly. The skipper called and asked my opinion on our options ahead. We were down to three thousand feet, and I replied that if we went southwest, we would fly into the mountains. If west, most of the Ruhr was in German hands and their flack would get us. If northwest, the Canadians would get us as their guns were set to fire on anything at three thousand feet or below to take care of the flying bombs. And flying northeast was over occupied Holland and the North Sea and we didn't care to swim.

"Prepare to abandon aircraft," Skipper ordered. Then he turned to me and said calmly that he'd like to get out of this and could I tie down his rudder pedal so he could trim the aircraft to fly straight and level. I did and it worked! We were down to two thousand feet. It was time to go.

I quickly put on my parachute, pulled up the escape hatch, and jumped out headfirst. Four others followed me and the gunners went out the back. I had to pull on my rip cord after just three seconds because we were so low. There was a great swish as the parachute opened, and I was amazed how quiet it was going down! Then I heard our aircraft crash and saw it burning. I hoped everyone got out.

In seconds, I was on my back on a tile roof, ten inches from the side, and my parachute was twisted around the chimney. It was now 11:35 p.m. and I was in the middle of Germany! My next thought was: *Is there an unhappy farmer around with a shotgun?* No one appeared. I was about ten feet off the ground, so I jumped down and started off.

Then I heard two blasts from a whistle. It was our mid-upper gunner, Curly, hiding behind a tree. There is a bit of humor in all of this as before Curly and the rear gunner jumped, they were on about something, so I asked Curly, who was semi-bald, what had been going on. It was quite simple. Curly had yelled back to the rear gunner to bring his hat because he didn't want to catch cold. But the rear gunner was nowhere near us now! Luckily, it was a mild night.

We carefully removed all the identification from our uniforms and started out. When we had been walking for some time, we heard trucks approaching. We had no idea if they were looking for us, but weren't about to wait to find out. Leaping down into a ditch filled with water, we spread-eagled ourselves just above the murky surface. The last thing we needed was to get sopping wet. As the trucks rumbled by, we didn't dare look up to see whether they were good guys or bad guys; we knew we'd get shot either way. We waited a few minutes, then crawled out and set off again. We looked for a place to hide. I pulled some boards off a shed, thinking maybe we could hunker down for an uneasy rest inside, but some wood tumbled out. Since that didn't work, we kept moving.

It was around 5 a.m. when we came upon a village. No one was in sight, but we were surprised by what we saw—white bedsheets hanging out of the windows and slung over the doors.

"They've surrendered," I said. I couldn't help but think, *Maybe we're okay.*

A bedsheet flapped from a flagpole in the square right in the middle of the village, and Curly shimmied up the pole and pulled down the flannel sheet. He was taking his chances with that stunt, but still no one appeared. We stowed the sheet away. Dawn was breaking, and with it came a great lot of noise—a motor pool or tanks warming up. I knew we had to find somewhere else to hide and quickly!

We made our way to the outskirts of a town and found a barn set back some distance. We were in luck. The chickens had just laid eggs, which we devoured. That was the first time I had raw eggs for breakfast, but they satisfied the worst of our hunger. We clambered up into the loft, which was filled with piles of warm, scratchy straw. I poked about and soon discovered a loose roof tile I could lift to peek outside. The farmer had emerged from his house, and I hoped he hadn't heard us over the clucking of the chickens. I took it as a good sign when he didn't have a shotgun on him. He turned almost immediately and went back into the house and didn't come back.

I peered out again from my little vantage point and spied a highway off in the distance. There were streams of people and tanks and trucks. The latter were emblazoned with stars.

"We're home free," I said. "They're Allies!" We scrambled down and ran out.

Refugees by the hundreds were hauling wagons and whatever else they could and had filled them with belongings. I tried to discover where they were coming from with what little German I knew.

Eventually, we arrived at an intersection where a military policeman was directing traffic. With some effort, I convinced him who we were and he called a jeep that took us to Osnabrück. I'd never seen anything like it. It was bombed out, with rubble on all sides. We went through to what had been a school—the name "Kindergarten" was on the building. We went into a tent where we sat down in front of a British army major of the British Second Army.

"What direction did you come from?" he asked.

I told him.

"Look at our tent," he said. It was filled with holes. "A few hours earlier, it was shot up by Hitler Youth. You walked through their territory and right through minefields. I think that I had better keep you out of any more trouble." He then summoned another jeep for us.

As we drove along the Dortmund–Ems Canal, a flash of red caught my eye in the only building standing near the town of Rheine.

"Stop!" I called out to the driver.

We made our way into the building, and I could see what I had spied from the outside. There were flags everywhere—swastikas, parade flags, and other insignia. I grabbed one large flag and some small flags. On the way out, we were stopped by a military policeman.

"Sir, what are you doing in there?"

"We're liberating these flags," I said, waving one of them.

"The building is booby-trapped!" he said.

I couldn't help but mutter to myself, "Stupid airman."

That's when the jeep driver said, "I'd better take you where you're supposed to go."

We ended up at a small air base at Burgsteinfurt where we met Air Commodore Boyle of the Royal Air Force (RAF) 2nd Tactical Air Force in support of the British Second Army. He asked us if we wanted to fly back to Holland with him. "I'll show you some of your work and some of our work along the way. But, you'll have to keep your eyes open as we aren't safe yet."

"I'm not going to fly anymore," Curly said.

"Well, I'll be damned if I'm going to walk anymore," I replied.

So, the air commodore and I took off on a great trip at two thousand feet above the Rhine River. He pointed out tanks that had been shot up by Typhoon aircraft and the city of Wesel—which was absolutely flattened—then we crossed the border and he flew me around the crumbled Philips Radio factory which had been the Gestapo headquarters in Eindhoven, Holland.

After our little tour, we landed on the first fairway of the golf course in our small aircraft. On entering the Golf Club, I was greeted by Group Captain Paul Davoud of Kingston, a friend of my brother. He made sure I got first-class treatment in Eindhoven and a trip back to England the very next day.

Back in England, I was escorted by a flight lieutenant in a private train coach to London to be interviewed by MI9. I knew MI9 well—they were military intelligence, the ones who trained us on evading and who set up all the escape routes in Europe. When we got to London, they quizzed me for two days. They replaced my grubby clothes with a new uniform, socks, shirt, and shoes, and I was fed well. When they were finally done with me, I made my way to air force headquarters and ran into yet another friend of the family, Corporal Jackson. Seems that Kingston men were everywhere!

I asked Jackson, "Am I dead or alive?"

"Wait a minute," he said, "let me check my files." He rifled through them. "You're dead."

"Oh, no!" I said, my heart sinking. "That means my parents got the telegram."

"Don't worry," Jackson replied, and he quickly sent a telegram to my parents saying that I was okay.

Unknown to me, my brother Sergeant Don was coming through London on his way to my squadron to pick up my personal effects, having received a telegram that I was missing. Guess what? Don ran into Corporal Jackson, who asked him where he was going.

Don replied, "I'm going to Stu's squadron to get his personal effects."

"Don't bother," Jackson told him. "I was speaking to him, and he is safe."

What about the premonition I'd had when I went to talk to the padre? And I also told my good friend Len about it. Normally, when aircrew go missing, airmen on the station will divide up their goodies, but Len had grabbed my gear and said, "You're not touching a thing. He'll be back!" And I was. In three days. Safe and sound! I later found out that the entire crew survived too.

During the war, we ran into an emergency, but we all did what we were supposed to do. Like everyone else in the war, we were just ordinary people doing what was expected of us. And we did it well!

The experience in the war made me feel like I could do things I never could before. Go back to school, do algebra and geometry and other subjects I wanted. Even go to university! I ended up working at the *Whig-Standard* again. First as a newspaper carrier and then as circulation manager. I am also a member of the Caterpillar Club, which means I saved my life by parachute.

Postscript: Postwar Kingston Connections

My brother Don, Group Captain Paul Davoud, and I had many coffee breaks at the restaurant next door to the *Whig-Standard*. Paul also kept me informed about Air Commodore Boyle, later Sir Dermot Boyle.

There were three former *Whig-Standard* paperboys on the squadron, and another was one of my customers. We all lived within blocks of each other and kept in touch postwar.

Our skipper, Hugh Cram, stayed in the air force and became the pilot for royalty as a wing commander. I spoke at his funeral in 2004.

Flying Officer Stuart Crawford (Ret) was born March 2, 1922, at home. He was a newspaper boy until he joined the Royal Canadian Air Force at age twenty. He served with the Canadian Air Force from August 1942 to September 1945. Stuart lives in Kingston, Ontario, with his wife, Mary.

Here I am in Britain in 1944.

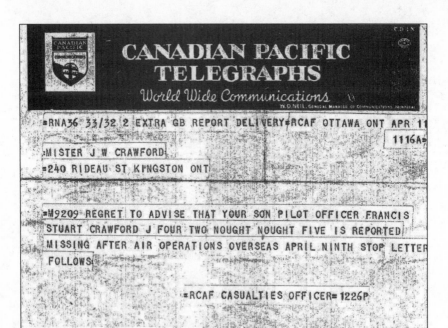

CANADIAN PACIFIC TELEGRAPHS
World Wide Communications
W.D. NEIL, GENERAL MANAGER OF COMMUNICATIONS, MONTREAL

=RNA36 33/32 2 EXTRA GB REPORT DELIVERY=RCAF OTTAWA ONT APR 11
1116A=

=MISTER J W CRAWFORD
=240 RIDEAU ST KINGSTON ONT

=M9209 REGRET TO ADVISE THAT YOUR SON PILOT OFFICER FRANCIS STUART CRAWFORD J FOUR TWO NOUGHT NOUGHT FIVE IS REPORTED MISSING AFTER AIR OPERATIONS OVERSEAS APRIL NINTH STOP LETTER FOLLOWS

=RCAF CASUALTIES OFFICER=1226P

My parents received this telegram after our Lancaster didn't return.

CANADIAN PACIFIC TELEGRAPHS
World Wide Communications
W.D. NEIL, GENERAL MANAGER OF COMMUNICATIONS, MONTREAL

RNA71 23/22 2 EXTRA GB REPORT DELIVERY=RCAF OTTAWA ONT APR
12 150P=

=MISTER J W CRAWFORD=
240 RIDEAU ST KINGSTON ONT=

M9307 PLEASED TO ADVISE THAT YOUR SON PILOT OFFICER FRANCIS STUART CRAWFORD HAS ARRIVED SAFELY UNITED KINGDOM STOP LETTER FOLLOWS=

A day after my parents were told I was MIA, this telegram was dispatched.

CANADIAN PACIFIC TELEGRAPHS
World Wide Communications
W. O. NEIL, General Manager of Communications Montreal

ra gr 25 Commercial XCI

                 Great Britain Apl 13 4pm

LC Mr and Mrs John Crawford
   240 RideauSt
   Kingston Ont.

   Dear Mother and Dad sorry to have caused all the

worry your loving son.

               Stuart Crawford

336pm

And I was sure to apologize for my absence.

FO. Crawford Safe in Britain

FO. Stuart Crawford, 22, son of Mr. and Mrs. John W. Crawford, 240 Rideau Street, who was reported missing after air operations overseas on April 9, has now been reported safe in the United Kingdom.

The young air force officer, who was formerly a Whig-Standard carrier, has been overseas one year. Educated at Robert Meek Public School and the KCVI, FO. Crawford was keenly interested in amateur photography and several of his pictures were published in The Whig-Standard. While at school, he also participated in sports and was an active member of Queen Street United Church.

He has one brother overseas, Flt. Sgt. Donald Crawford, while another brother, Lieut. Jack Crawford, recently received his discharge from the Canadian Army. A younger brother, Malcolm, who has the paper route at present, is at home.

The *Whig-Standard* ran an article about my ordeal. I would go on to work for the paper for thirty-seven years.

A Regular Job

FLYING OFFICER NOEL SHANKS (RET)

*I knew that as a tail gunner I was a target for the
Germans. My chances of surviving were about 15
percent, but it's funny, once we were airborne,
I never thought I would be shot down.*

I was born in 1922 and grew up in Sharbot Lake, Ontario, with
three brothers and three sisters. My parents named me Noel because I was born on Christmas Day. Once I finished high school,
I decided to join the Royal Canadian Air Force (RCAF). The war
had already started, and I didn't want to get stuck in the army. I was
looking for clean sheets. I was a skinny kid, but like all young lads,
I wanted to be in the war effort, and I wanted to get into the war
before it ended.

Unfortunately, the RCAF wouldn't take me. However, they took
my name and told me they'd contact me when I turned eighteen.
While I waited for that call, I went to work for an aluminum company
in Kingston, Ontario. In January 1942, the air force got in touch by
telegram and told me to report.

They sent me to Lachine, a depot for new recruits. It was February, wintertime, and I spent a lot of my hours shoveling snow off the aircrafts that were parked there and waiting to fly to England.

When I came before the Air Board, they asked me what I would like to be. One of my brothers was a pilot and another was a navigator. They knew what I was going to say, but they asked anyway.

"I'd like to be a pilot," I answered.

"We've got lots of pilots," they said. "But we're awful short on tail gunners. Would you like to be a tail gunner?"

"How long do I have to think about it?" I asked.

"Now."

"Okay." I had dreams that maybe I would get a posting to Bermuda or some place like that, but the real godsend was that I was getting airborne. I was shipped off for training, and then in August, I went to Halifax and boarded the *Queen Mary* along with three thousand other troops and went to England.

Because of my gunnery training, I was recruited by the crew of the ship to keep my eyes open for enemy submarines, as radar wasn't around yet. We were coming up the east coast of Nova Scotia, and I said to the Royal Navy chap who was there, "You know, there's a submarine out there." And he turned to me, just as the object I had my eye on was sinking down, and said, "Ah, no, that's just a whale." But the funny thing was, within minutes, the ship changed to starboard directly, so it had to have been a German submarine.

When we arrived in England, we went to Bournemouth, where all the Canadian air force members went, and they decided I would be transferred to the RAF. At that time, the RAF had a whole bunch of Canadians—maybe even more than British. I remember being in a large auditorium, and there were a bunch of gunners in one corner, navigators in another, and radio operators in another. And a pilot came around, and he just picked out whoever he wanted to make up his Lancaster bombing crew: pilot, flight engineer, navigator, bomb aimer, radio operator, mid-upper gunner, and rear gunner.

He stopped in front of me and asked, "How would you like to fly with me?"

I was desperate so I said, "Okay!" and that's how I got in with a real good crew.

After several months of more training, I was posted to RAF 115 Squadron, 3 Group, led by Flight Lieutenant Stanley Garside, at Witchford, Cambridgeshire.

Being on a real squadron was like having a regular job. We were just going to work. Each morning, I would check the blackboard outside the mess. It had all the pilots' last names that were scheduled to operate that night. If I saw Garside, then I'd take the afternoon off and come back at 5 p.m. for a nice meal, then at seven I'd head to the auditorium, where all the crews for that night's operation would assemble. The commanding officer for the unit would come in, we'd stand and salute him, and then he'd pull the covering off the map of Europe that hung at the end of the room. That's when I'd hear groans as about 150 people found out where they'd be flying.

We'd be briefed on the weather, our routes, and how much enemy fire they expected on our way to the target. After twenty minutes, we'd get our flying equipment and climb into the back of an ordinary truck with wooden benches with four other crews and get dropped off in front of our Lancaster bomber.

In our squadron, if the operation was a "go," they'd shoot a green rocket. If it was cancelled, we'd see a red one go up—but I don't think I ever saw a red rocket. Each fellow in our crew would climb into his position, and Stan would fire up the four engines and we'd taxi out for takeoff with the other twenty-two aircraft. We'd wait our turn, then pull around and do the "run-up." Our survival rate was fifty-fifty.

Stan would say, "Okay, let's go," and turn to the flight engineer, a guy we called Mac, and say, "Now, when I press on the throttles forward, you put your hands on mine and press. Don't let me pull the power off until I tell you." That way, he wouldn't be inclined to reduce power, and we needed all the power we could get to get airborne.

There wasn't radar on our Lancaster at the time, so as the tail gunner, all I did was sit in that little cupola at the back end of the Lanc and stare out into the darkness for five or six hours. The turret was beyond the tail of the aircraft, and I could look back, up, and sideways, and I had a pretty good view forward too. Sometimes I removed the clear Plexiglas shield in the rear of my turret—it made it very cold inside, but I could spot planes better. If I saw any aircraft, I would advise Stan. I'd say, "There's an aircraft sitting back there. Can't tell if it's another Lanc or a German fighter." I was the only one with that kind of view. I was the eyes of the crew, helping us avoid any encounters with German fighter planes. I knew that as a tail gunner I was a target for the Germans. My chances of surviving were about 15 percent, but it's funny, once we were airborne, I never thought I would be shot down.

It was incredibly loud inside the Lancaster. We were hooked up with a PA system, but no one ever talked unless they had to. All you could hear was Stan and Mac controlling the engines. We'd stare down to see if we were over the right city, looking for the fires that indicated our targets. The Germans were great for starting another fire someplace close by, and a lot of people would bomb the wrong target. Soon, we'd be tasked with one of the most important targets of all.

———

On June 5, 1944, the crews for that night's operation ambled into the auditorium for our briefing. We were told our target was Ouistreham in Normandy, but I didn't know how to spell it so I wrote OP CAEN in my logbook. It seemed like any other trip, but the commander did say that we would see a lot of sea and air traffic, but to keep our eyes open and fly above ten thousand feet. We were later told that the navy had been ordered to shoot down any aircraft below that altitude.

There were 1,025 Lancasters in the sky, and as usual, we all flew with no lights. The only time we turned on the lights was when we were landing on the runway on return. We flew over Sword Beach and bombed our target, a large German gun installation at Ouistreham. On our way back, I remember looking down and seeing the British troops, the 3rd British Infantry Division, in their small boats going ashore. In the back of the Lancaster, I could see the view for a long time. We never thought that this was D-Day. We flew back to base, had breakfast, and went to bed.

At four o'clock, I woke up and went outside. The first airman I saw said to me, "The real war has started." I found the crew, and they told me that we were on again, to get ready to go. And we made a second trip that night.

For three days, the newspapers in England didn't say anything, so no one knew the invasion had started, except for the commanders in the know. They wanted to keep what we were doing a secret from the Germans, who thought we'd invade much farther north on the coast of France.

Before D-Day, I had been on four trips; after, I went on to do twenty-five more.

One night when we were out, all of a sudden we heard the sound of bullets striking our Lanc as a German fighter strafed us. We had holes in our wings and we were plummeting down to earth. We had to get straightened out before we could come back up, but we were in danger of our wings snapping off. We were hurtling over four hundred miles per hour, and at nine thousand feet, we recovered, and all I lost was a pair of spare gloves. The crew I flew with was very good.

One of my worst trips was bombing Kiel in Germany. We had flown low level from England and we didn't climb until late in the operation, and as we came over Kiel, we saw that the bombing was very intense. I'd never seen such fireworks in all my life. The bombing was so severe that as soon as the bombs were dropped, Stan had to do a diving turn to get out of it. As he turned to the left, the movement of the aircraft was so quick that it toppled all the compasses. So we were flying thinking that we were heading for England, but we were really just flying in a big circle. We flew over Germany and they started taking shots at us. We managed to get straightened out and made it back home. I found out later that the brother of a girl I had left in Montreal had been killed during that raid.

I suppose I was scared sometimes, but it didn't register. And what I was involved in never bothered me. I was born lucky. In mid-August 1944, I finished my thirtieth mission, then stayed in England resting up and instructing for a year until I was assigned to a Canadian air force squadron for a second tour, in the Far East. On my way back to Canada, the A-bomb was dropped and the war ended shortly after. I was home for good. All three of my brothers returned from the war as well.

I must say I did enjoy my service. I'm sure glad I flew with the RAF. They knew there was a war that had to be won and they dedicated themselves to it. I had three wonderful years with them, then sixty-two wonderful years with my wife, Eileen.

I've really had a perfect life. I can't think of a day I didn't enjoy. I'm an old, old man but I can still remember something good and smile about it.

Postscript

On May 6, 2017, Noel passed away. He is remembered fondly by his loved ones as a kind gentleman who always had a positive attitude and a smile on his face. His favourite pastimes included reading *The Globe and Mail* and the *National Post*, making homemade jam, tinkering with clocks, and spending time with friends and family. He was thankful for the many blessings in his life. As a proud Canadian, Noel flew a Canadian flag on his front lawn.

Flying Officer Noel Shanks (Ret) was born on Christmas Day in 1922. He joined the RCAF in 1942 as a tail gunner and was transferred to the RAF in England. He flew thirty missions with RAF Squadron 115, 3 Group, including two raids during the D-Day invasion on June 6, 1944. He met and married his wife, Eileen, during his employment at Air Canada.

Noel and the aircrew of Squadron 115 in front of their Lancaster. He's third from the right.

Noel with his logbook. He loved to share memories about his wartime experiences.

Noel with CBC News anchor Peter Mansbridge at the Canadian Warplane Heritage Museum near Hamilton, Ontario, home to one of the last two operating Lancasters in the world. *The National* aired a documentary on the Lancaster bomber for the seventieth anniversary of D-Day, and Noel shared his story.

Noel with his good friend and neighbour Jacob Long at Pineland Public School in Burlington, Ontario, on Remembrance Day 2016. Every year Noel would visit the school to lay a wreath in memory of those who gave their lives and to chat with the children.

A Writer's View of "The Wavy Navy"

Writer J. W. (Bill) Fitsell (Ret)

I was gung-ho but naïve.
This was an adventure and I didn't know any better.

I was born in Barrie, Ontario, in 1923. I was named John after my father and Walter after another army veteran, my Uncle "Wal," but my mother, the youngest of a family of ten, liked the name of another brother, William, and so I grew up being called "Bill."

When I was a young child, my family moved to Lindsay, where I served in the Collegiate Institute Cadet Corps and as a "Tuesday-night gunner" in the 56th Battery, a reserve unit, and every Tuesday I would train with the artillery.

During the first years of World War II, I saw a film feature at the local cinema about the glories of sailing the ocean waters in the Canadian navy, and I was intrigued. I was almost eighteen and knew I would be called to volunteer soon, but I didn't particularly like the local army reserve unit. So, in 1942, I went with a group of four teenagers to the armed forces recruiting centres at the Toronto Exhibition grounds. We went our separate ways, and I enlisted in the Royal Canadian Naval Volunteer Reserve (RCNVR) at HMCS York.

Everyone was joining up, including my father, who served as a signaller in the army during the first war and survived the Battle of Vimy Ridge. Over the next two years, my younger brother Stan would also join the army, and my youngest brother, Frank, a Boy Scout, would sign up with the Sea Cadets. It was the thing to do. My parents were English, so we knew we were going to support both their homeland of Britain and our home in Canada.

At HMCS York, we did our basic training: learned that the floor was called "deck" and the wall, "bulkhead"—all the naval language going back to the Royal Navy of Britain. We did our marching to the RCNVR tune "Roll Along, Wavy Navy, Roll Along," and got into routine, then we shipped out to Esquimalt, British Columbia, to get our trade training. My rank as a rating was probationary writer, and I served under the captain and pay officer. "Rating" is the word used in the navy that's equivalent to airman in the air force or soldier in the army.

As a writer or scribe, my action station was the plot cabin just forward of the bridge and the wheelhouse. I manned a glass-topped table with a light underneath that automatically followed the ship's course. I'd mark our course on the paper chart above and take reports from nearby ASDIC (Sonar) operators listening for German submarines. I'd add radar reports of aircraft and other ships and record the positions so that the gunnery officer could survey the situation and report to the duty officer. If the ASDIC operators did identify a "blip," as they called it, we would monitor and chart it. As we got closer to the target, the captain would drop by the plot cabin and determine if the blip was an enemy submarine, a wreck on the bottom of the ocean, or just a school of fish. If it was the former, we'd drop depth charges.

While part of my job was to handle the plot, my main, everyday task was to man the ship's office and maintain the records. This included the King's Regulations and Admiralty Instructions (K.R. & A.I.) book from the Royal Navy, which we nicknamed "K.R. & F.U."

I also handled the crew's pay allotments and requests. Every time the ship left port, my last duty was to update a list of everyone on board—a detailed roster of names, ranks, and serial numbers—in case anything unfortunate happened while we were at sea. It was important for me to know every member of the crew. And that's how I met sterling seamen, stokers, coders, and gunners from all across Canada—the Prairies, northern Ontario, both coasts, and downtown Montreal.

After six months in B.C., I was posted to Halifax, where HMCS *St. Francis*, an old American destroyer—one of the six given to Canada in return for naval bases—was under refit. I had just turned twenty and was eager to get to sea. It was why I joined the navy in the first place! I replaced the veteran writer aboard, who had had enough of sea duty and was glad to get ashore.

St. Francis had been serving on the Atlantic for a couple of years, so I was lucky to move into a very experienced crew with at least six permanent-force RCN veterans in key positions—the rest of us were volunteer reserves, or VRs. The permanent-force vets had signed up in the 1930s and the navy was a lifetime job for them; for us, we volunteered to serve "for the duration of the war." We were trained quickly and assigned to overseas convoy duty. With four or five other vessels, we escorted Britain-bound merchant ships that ran the Atlantic Ocean gauntlet against the German U-boats.

The bane of many sailors on small ships in rough seas was nausea, and I was no different. If seasick pills failed, one antidote was to do "funnel watch" on the breezy upper deck, which meant we'd sit with our backs to the warm funnels or smokestacks and try and still our stomachs. It helped us avoid, as some wags quipped, "travelling the Atlantic by rail," that is, grabbing on to the railing of the ship and upchucking. I fought off queasiness by "crashing" or getting my head down, and soon earned the nickname "Horizontal," which was all part of the good-natured repartee among mates.

St. Francis had bunks for about 90 men, but we had about 150 sailors on board, so we took turns sleeping. When I came off watch, I would look around for an empty bunk and get my snooze time wherever I could. We were bunked in messes, and I was welcomed in the communications mess with the telegraphers and the signallers. This was great because I was constantly looking for news and always asking, "What's the buzz?" Between what the tels and sigs could provide and what I overheard from the captain and other officers, I would join the other sailors in trying to answer the key question: "When is the ship going to return to Canada?" Each mess would have a lottery and try to pick the date. It was one of the games we played to while away the hours. The pot was always a small amount, maybe a few pounds sterling. I would have a pretty good idea of the date because of my inside information, but I don't think I ever was spot-on.

As was the custom in the Royal Navy, "kye" was served to crew members coming off night watch. This steaming hot chocolate was delivered throughout the ship in a tall metal container by a duty man. One night it was placed on our mess deck table. The St. Francis was particularly narrow-beamed and rolled in high seas. I was sitting with my knees up in front of me when the ship lurched and the cocoa tipped over and the kye spilled down my shins. I got quite a burn, but was quickly medicated and bandaged by "the Tiffy"—a well-trained sick bay attendant. That was the only scratch I ever got. How lucky can one get?

Our ship was capable of doing twenty-one knots (about seventeen or eighteen miles an hour), and on my first "all expenses cruise across the North Atlantic" we had good weather conditions and reached Londonderry in Northern Ireland within a week without incident.

But our trip back wasn't as speedy, and tensions were high as our sister ship, HMCS St. Croix, was reported sunk. Enemy activity forced us to travel north from Ireland to Iceland, along the coast of Greenland, then down to Newfoundland and our home port in Halifax. We were twenty-one days returning and nearly ran out of supplies. I remember cutting one of the last hunks of mouldy brown bread down to a centre core and eating it—with relish!

Despite our low supplies, I was never worried about running out of food. I was gung-ho but naïve. This was an adventure and I didn't know any better, unlike some of the older seamen who sometimes showed signs of stress or got into their illegal rum cache in the middle of the ocean.

After we returned from Londonderry, the new Canadian frigates were coming on line, and in late 1943 I was assigned with all crew members except the stokers to the Quebec-built HMCS *Outremont*. On the next trip overseas, our escort group of six frigates was trained as an antisubmarine strike force—seeking out U-boats before they could attack. Despite what you might think, antisub work wasn't as dangerous as convoy duty, because when we were escorting ships we had to travel at the speed of the slowest merchant ships. Even though we still did the same routine jobs, it was a little more exciting to think we were hunting subs. We were young and full of beans and enthusiasm.

At this time, the navy was getting better at tracking U-boats. The first WRCNSs (Women's Royal Canadian Naval Service), or Wrens, had joined the all-male navy and served at shore bases listening and decoding the German messages about U-boat activity. They worked in conjunction with "Huff Duffers"—high-frequency direction-finder telegraphists on ships—who could obtain a fix on U-boat positions and directions.

In April 1944, our group was assigned to protect a U.K. convoy heading with armaments and supplies for Murmansk, Russia, which was a hot spot at that time. I was reassigned from the plot to depth-charge watch on the quarterdeck. Outfitted in a new zippered ski suit, fur hat, and mitts, I kept warm on the quarterdeck by sparring with the other sailors. My dad had taught me how to box, so I was in good stead against my fellow sailors, even the six-foot-one Prince Edward Islander we had on board. I knew how to protect my chin with my left glove and have my right ready, but it was all done in good fun. As for the depth charges, luckily we didn't have to set and fire any, although the sixty-ship convoy paced to the slowest merchant ship and we did hear of a few ships sunk during our journey. But they were far from our location in the convoy.

The real joy of that trip was being able to get ashore in Vaenga, meet the Russians, and barter for souvenirs. The most coveted was a Russian Red Star—reportedly made out of aluminum from airplanes that had been shot down in the Finnish-Russian war just a few years before. I got one, but I must have traded it away.

We explored the small community and even got to enjoy a film, *How Green Was My Valley*, despite the operators switching two of the reels, which we had to figure out.

On our return from above the Arctic Circle, we visited the Danish Faeroe Islands and later got in on some night action. U-boat 1006 was just a week out from Norway, occupied by Germany at the time, and our group attacked the sub. We didn't play a vital role—only adding illumination for the attack—but we did take on twenty-seven survivors. The German sailors were very young and inexperienced because the Nazis were getting short of men and losing lots of submarines, so these men were a rather ragtag crew that had been recruited and trained recently.

As writer, I was selected to get their names, ranks, and serial numbers for the official record. I went down to the stokers' mess in the lower section of the ship, where they were being held. A seaman with a submachine gun stood at the entrance of the mess. This was my first time seeing the enemy face-to-face, and while there was some tension, I didn't feel intimidated. The prisoners were dressed in old clothes and survival gear, and they looked almost happy to be caught and out of the war. I started taking down their information including ages, but I was having trouble, and one of the Germans could see this. He took my pencil and wrote the names down in broad Germanic style for me. I still have it.

We took the POWs into Glasgow, Scotland, and when they were going off the ship, the German captain gave the Nazi salute. We didn't really like that because that gesture represented all the worst parts of the enemy. We didn't scream or yell, just hissed at the affront. Years later, our captain met and conversed with this German commander at a NATO meeting in Montreal. That's how war changes allegiances and associations over the years; this German captain was no longer an enemy.

In June 1944, we moved down the Irish Sea to Anglesey, Wales, tucked in under the west coast of England. It was a huge harbour. I saw six ships come in and anchor, and then another six ships, and I said, "Something is going on here." Soon enough the whole bay was full of warships. I guess I had a touch of history even then because I surveyed the scene and put my thoughts on paper.

On the night of June 4, there was a storm and our ship dragged anchor. On the fifth, we sailed out southward to the English Channel, and the next day on the American Forces radio network, we heard General Eisenhower, the head of the Allied Forces, announce: "This is it. This is D-Day," and the long awaited invasion began.

We were excited. This was it. This was what we were waiting for, what we'd trained for—to end the war and go home, back to civilian life. Some of the troops had been training in England for years, waiting for this moment. We knew that this operation was a step towards peace.

Our escort group moved on patrol from Land's End in England to the Bay of Biscay in France to help block off German U-boats from the invasion area. When the Allied Forces pretty well bottled up the subs, we moved into the channel and got a view of the French coast. We saw the huge armada of ships and planes moving towards the beaches. When we saw the explosions in the night sky, we felt blessed to be safe while many heroic Canadians, Americans, and British were dying on those beaches.

We didn't have to wait long for action ourselves. Four days after D-Day, I woke up in my hammock and looked down to the mess deck below to see a whole bunch of strange sailors sitting around. The aircraft carrier *Tracker*, which we were escorting, had collided in the inky blackness with the British-built frigate HMCS *Teme* and almost cut it in half. We had picked up seventy-three ratings, bunked seven in our mess, and towed the badly damaged frigate into Barry Road, near Cardiff, Wales. Our captain, a veteran of the merchant service, received a special commendation for the seamanship skills performed in salvaging the ship. *Teme* was eventually repaired and returned to action.

After that incident and a false report of a U-boat on the surface, we patrolled the eastern section of the channel, and saw the famous White Cliffs of Dover, not far from my father's hometown of Hastings. Strangely enough, the weather had turned beautiful. It was sunny and calm, and the off-duty guys had time to sun themselves on the deck. It reminded me of the World War I song: "Oh, oh, oh, it's a lovely war!" The irony of the moment wasn't lost on me. Here we were enjoying the sun and calm waters, and meanwhile a war was going on.

The Americans had good radio programs, so we were able to listen to the BBC and even got the odd hockey broadcast from Canada. And we were able to keep up with the advancement of our troops from France into Holland. Their progress cheered us up immensely. We had an idea of what they were going through, but every advancement meant we were closer to victory. In some small way we were contributing. We even started a newspaper on board ship. The telegraphists would copy shortwave news reports, and I would type them out and present them in a two- to four-page newsletter for the crew. We called it the *Outremont Oracle*.

We patrolled throughout the summer and fall, and occasionally were treated to fresh seafood dinners from fish brought to the surface by depth charge explosions. The channel was very shallow, so there were many false echoes off old wrecks.

As the action waned, we were granted leave in British naval ports. The first thing we saw when we went ashore were the damaged homes on Plymouth Hoe. We were shocked. The homes were rubble; only foundations were left. We knew people had died there, and the sight of the aftermath really hit home with us and we were impressed by the spirit of the U.K. people.

At Portsmouth we were given a Royal Navy tour of Vice Admiral Horatio Nelson's HMS *Victory* and told tales of days of "wooden ships and iron men." The navy in Nelson's days was much tougher, and the new version was that the navy was now full of "wooden men and iron ships."

Late in 1945, we came back to Canada. I moved to Sydney, Nova Scotia, and signed up for the war in the Pacific theatre—another "for the duration" deal. Before going on an extended leave, I met a beautiful young lady on the dance floor named Barbara Robson. She wanted to jitterbug, but I did a version of the foxtrot. As the story goes, she said, "Don't tell me I'm stuck with this guy all night." So I learned the jitterbug and the rest is history. Seventy-two years later we still share this story.

While the dockyard mateys were refitting the ship for the Pacific, the Americans dropped the atomic bomb and the war ended in Japan. That cleared the way for the love of my life and I to be married. I was posted to a discharge base in Halifax and served there until February 1946.

Then I picked up my bride and entrained to Lindsay, where we went on to greater things—blessed with five fine daughters and twenty-one grandchildren, including three great-great granddaughters. We're still happily together and counting our many blessings.

When I was being released from service, the Canadian Legion sent out information about postwar careers for veterans. I always wanted to be in the newspaper business, so I wrote my hometown paper, the *Daily Post*. I had an interview with the publisher and a few days later started to work as a rookie reporter. After gaining more experience in Ontario weeklies and dailies, I settled down in the historic city of Kingston, and served the *Whig-Standard* as bureau chief, district editor, and columnist for thirty years. That's where I met my good friend Stu Crawford, a modest veteran of the RCAF. We often talk about how lucky we were to have served and survived.

At ninety-four, I look back on my life with contentment and humble pride.

Writer J. W. (Bill) Fitsell (Ret) joined the Royal Canadian Navy in 1942 and served at sea on the *St. Francis* and the *Outremont* until 1946. He gained reporting skills at several Ontario daily and weekly newspapers and finished his fifty-year news career with the *Whig-Standard*. He served the International Hockey Hall of Fame and Museum as curator, secretary, president, and historian. Bill is the founding president of the Society for International Hockey Research (SIHR) and has written four books on hockey history. In 2006, the worldwide research group honoured him with the Brian McFarlane Award for outstanding research and writing. He retains his naval interest as a member of HMCS Cataraqui Association in Kingston, Ontario, where he lives with his beloved wife, Barbara.

My first uniform, issued in 1943.

The gold thread badge worn on the right arm of my "Tiddly" (walking-out) uniform. The *W* is for Writer—not Warrior.

Waiting to go ashore on leave in England before returning home to Canada. I'm on the quarterdeck of the *Outremont*; the depth charges are behind me.

The HMCS *Outremont* in the harbour in Sydney, Nova Scotia, in 1945. She was being refitted before our tour in the Pacific. Luckily, the war ended before we had to go.

Barbara and me on our wedding day, October 12, 1945. Barbara's brother, Jack Robson (*far left*), was with the Cape Breton Highlanders and served for three years in Germany. He made it back just a few months before our wedding.

I'm privileged to be able to share my experiences from my navy days. Here I am at HMCS Cataraqui, Kingston, in 2015, with my medals—including the Atlantic Star, which I received for my WWII service.

THE KOREAN WAR

Defending Hill 667, the Battle of Kapyong

PRIVATE MICHAEL CZUBOKA (RET)

*About halfway across the stormy Pacific, we were told
that the Chinese had entered Korea in large numbers
and that the United Nations forces were in retreat.
We were going to a full-scale war and not occupation
duties as previously announced.*

I was born in Brandon, Manitoba, to Ukrainian immigrant parents
in 1931. My father, a CN section labourer, like thousands of other
Ukrainians, came to Canada to gain freedom from an oppressive and
foreign regime. But during WWI, he was unjustly interned by Canadian authorities simply because he was classified as a citizen of the
Austrian-Hungarian Empire. Although he was probably never able
to overcome his belief that he was an unwanted foreigner in Canada,
I believe that he wanted me and my two brothers to be good Canadians. As a young man, I felt I needed to prove this too. I greatly ad-
mired my older brother, Walter, who served as a flying officer with the
Royal Canadian Air Force during WWII, and I couldn't help but feel
that I had missed out on a great historical event.

Little did I know that the kind of adventure I wished for was just
around the corner.

In June 1950, the Korean War broke out, and the government announced that it would recruit a "Special Force" for the purpose of serving in the war, and the period of service would be limited to eighteen months instead of the usual three years. So in early August, at eighteen, I decided to travel from my home in Rivers to Fort Osborne in Winnipeg, a distance of about 125 miles, in order to join up. But I didn't have enough money. Fortunately, I knew a CN Railway fireman, and he smuggled me into a caboose at the end of a freight train going to Winnipeg. I arrived full of enthusiasm but was met with skepticism. The recruiting officer told me that I needed to be nineteen to join the Special Force and told me to come back in a year.

I did go back to Rivers, but I returned to Fort Osborne two weeks later and hesitatingly, and with considerable trepidation, told a different recruiting officer that I was nineteen. Instantly, I aged by one year and was enrolled, at my request, in the Princess Patricia's Canadian Light Infantry (PPCLI). I wanted adventure, and the infantry was the place to get it.

I joined the 2nd Battalion, PPCLI of the 25th Infantry Brigade as a rifleman and was equipped with a WWII vintage uniform and a .303 Lee-Enfield rifle. Under the command of Lieutenant Colonel "Big Jim" Stone and Brigadier John Rockingham, who had both served with distinction in WWII, our company trained in Wainwright, Alberta, before moving to better facilities in Fort Lewis, Seattle. We were excited to train in a large American city, which, we reasoned, was sure to have a lot of beautiful women to consort with handsome and heroic Canadian soldiers. But shortly after our arrival in Fort Lewis, the Canadian government decided that only our battalion would be sent to Korea on an immediate basis.

An ocean away, the Communist forces of North Korea had been pushed back to the Yalu River on the border with China, and General Douglas MacArthur, the United Nations commander, had declared that the war would be over by Christmas. It appeared that 2nd Battalion,

PPCLI was being sent as a token occupation force and that the rest of the brigade would probably not follow. Immediately, we were reassigned. Instead of remaining in my rifle company, I was told that I would be joining the mortar platoon. I was actually quite pleased with this new assignment because it meant riding in a vehicle rather than marching on foot with a rifle and heavy supplies. I suspect that I was chosen for the mortar platoon because of my grade-twelve education. Most soldiers of that era did not have a high school standing, and mortar men needed to learn more technical skills than riflemen. But I didn't know anything about mortars and wouldn't see any 81mm mortars until after we arrived in Korea. That's how the army worked in those days.

On November 25, after only four days at Fort Lewis, we were shipped to Port Angeles and loaded onto the *Private J. P. Martinez*, a rusting "liberty ship" from WWII. These vessels had been welded together for temporary use and did not appear to be very seaworthy. The facilities were crude and the food was almost inedible. We had coloured meal cards and ate at badly coordinated times to announcements on loudspeakers such as: "Yellow cards will chow now." The weather was some of the worst in memory; even the ship's crew were seasick. I spent the first week in my bunk flat on my back and next to my rifle. About halfway across the stormy Pacific, we were told that the Chinese had entered Korea in large numbers and that the United Nations forces were in retreat. We were going to a full-scale war and not occupation duties as previously announced.

On December 18, we arrived in the "land of the morning calm" and disembarked to the sounds of a welcoming U.S. military band. Our commander, Big Jim Stone, immediately advised General Walker, his American superior, that we were not ready to fight and needed about six weeks of training. We were moved to an orchard area near Miryang, about 50 km north of Pusan, and that's where I learned how to use an 81mm mortar.

I was assigned to a number two position; it was my responsibility to feed bombs or shells into my mortar. This required good coordination because a "double feed" into a barrel would cause an explosion and wipe out the whole mortar crew, as happened on more than one occasion. A double feed occurred when a mortar shell was inserted into the mortar barrel too quickly, before the first shell had exited. If the two shells met inside the barrel they would explode. We determined range with an elevation-finding sight on the side of the mortar. Small packages of explosives called "charges" were added or removed at the end of each bomb for the purpose of increasing or decreasing distances of delivery.

Our platoon had six half-tracks with a three-man mortar crew each. A half-track was like a regular vehicle, except at the back, instead of wheels, there were continuous tracks to carry most of the load. Each half-track had one .50-caliber and one .30-caliber machine gun mounted. We carried several hundred bombs, most of which were of the high-explosive variety and a few that were made of phosphorus and used for creating smoke.

In the middle of February 1951, our battalion was loaded onto trucks and half-tracks at Miryang in preparation for our move to the front, at that time about 200 km to the north. I remember the cloudy skies, snow-covered valleys and mountains, icy and winding roads, and the bitter sub-zero cold. It took us about two days to get from Miryang to the front. Very cold arctic winds from nearby Siberia often descend down the Korean Peninsula, and they certainly came frequently in the winter of 1950–51.

As we arrived on our half-tracks at the Korean village of Kudun, near the front line, we were suddenly confronted with a scene of horror—a multitude of dead and naked bodies were scattered all around us. They were black American soldiers. The Chinese had bayonetted and shot them while they slept, then removed their weapons and clothing. Apparently these American soldiers had posted a single sentry on the previous evening and had not dug slit trenches. Although only about sixty-eight bodies were counted on that day, it was subsequently reported that more than two hundred had been killed. In later years I read a report by the Chinese Communist Forces (CCF) 116th Division claiming that two companies of the U.S. 23rd Infantry Regiment had been annihilated at dawn on February 14, 1951.

I was shocked by this bloody spectacle and ate very little for the next several days. I knew that we were in a war, but I was not prepared for such a sudden and violent introduction. I noticed that my three companions on our half-track were also taking it badly. Big Jim Stone, on the other hand, considered this to be an important lesson for all of us. We would, in future, never be allowed to use sleeping bags in the front line because they were hard to get out of quickly in the event of an attack. And needless to say, it became apparent that a strong contingent of sentries was always needed, and especially at dawn, the time when the Chinese preferred to attack.

The first year in Korea was one of rapid movement. Seoul was retaken in mid-March, and the UN forces, including our battalion, began to push across the 38th parallel and into North Korea.

In April we were in a reserve position in Kapyong, busy cleaning weapons, undergoing kit inspections, and replenishing ammunition and other supplies, unaware that the South Koreans and British forces were being wiped out nearby. All we knew was that the Chinese were attacking in large numbers—the Chinese Spring Offensive—and that we would have to stop them. I was not particularly afraid of this development, and I think my colleagues felt the same way. This was another battle just like the others. We were not aware of the seriousness of this situation.

Suddenly, we were ordered to take positions on Hill 677 across from the 3rd Battalion of the Royal Australian Regiment on Hill 504. The valley below was a critical part of the main route to the South

Korean capital of Seoul, and the Chinese knew they needed to control Hills 677 and 504 to allow a safe passage southward.

Before our company headed out, Lieutenant Colonel Stone took the commanders, including Captain Lloyd Hill, my 81mm mortar platoon commander, on a reconnaissance of Hill 677 to study the approaches that the Chinese would likely use during their attack.

The advantage of Hill 677 was that it contained many very steep approaches, which meant that our attackers would have to monkey run upwards to get at us. In those days the mountains of Korea had very few trees and visibility was unrestricted, making the Chinese especially vulnerable to grenades rolling down the steep and visible slopes. But given the geography, the defense of Hill 677 would largely depend upon artillery and 81mm mortar fire.

Under the cover of darkness, we ascended Hill 677 with heavily loaded half-tracks. Ours was so full that we were forced to sit haphazardly on top of our heavy and volatile load. A single enemy shell or rocket could easily have instantly detonated the whole load and blown all of us to kingdom come. It was difficult to see anything in the blackness around us, and the route was a single narrow trail that wound dangerously back and forth on its way to the summit. A slide into one of the deep ravines that bordered the trail would have been disastrous. In some places the trail was blocked with large stone outcrops, and we had to stop and blow them away with explosives. Then, when we were almost at the top, one of our half-tracks broke down. Lieutenant Colonel Stone threatened to push it into a nearby ravine, but fortunately a mechanic, Bob Hoffman, revived the vehicle, which had apparently stopped because of a dead battery.

Soon after arriving near the top of Hill 677, we unloaded our mortars and set them up in small rice paddies. The ground was very hard, and it was impossible to dig down more than a few inches. However, the rice paddies, with their stone walls, did offer some protection. My number one, Robbie Roberts, and I unloaded all two thousand

mortar bombs in a pile close to our mortar. The whole platoon probably hauled about twelve thousand mortar bombs to the top of Hill
677. The other five mortars were set up similarly on rice paddies that
were close to ours, and I dismounted the .30-caliber machine gun
from our half-track to provide additional protection, which gave me
a strong sense of security. We knew we were in a precarious situation,
and excitement filled the air.

We were assigned defensive fire tasks. This allowed us to zero in
on the places where the Chinese were likely to attack. These targets
were called Fox 1, Fox 2, Fox 3, and so on.

During that first night, hundreds of shadowy figures poured past
us in a southerly direction. We were told that these usually weapon-
less men were remnants of the Republic of Korea 6th Division, but
we were not sure. They could have been Chinese and North Koreans,
and it is entirely possible that some of them were indeed our enemies.
Infiltration was a common Communist tactic. These unwelcome in-
truders sometimes came to within fifty metres of our position and
they made us extremely nervous.

Then we sat and waited. The Chinese attacked the Australians
on Hill 504 first, and from our position high on Hill 677 we had a
grandstand view of the battle. Large numbers of Chinese soldiers
were seen amassing in the valley below. Several American tanks were
engaged in the battle and one was knocked out. The Americans performed heroically even though they were engulfed by the swarming
Chinese who overran Hill 504 and forced the Australians to withdraw. We were now alone, and the Chinese turned their attention in
our direction.

The first attacks were against Baker Company, approximately two
hundred metres to the northeast of our position, during the night of
April 23. Able, Charlie, and Dog Companies were situated in higher
isolated positions to the north and west of Baker and farther away
from the river valley.

Although we were close to Baker Company and could hear all of the violent battle noises, we did not, at that time, know about the hand-to-hand fighting that was taking place. The Chinese played bugles prior to their attacks, apparently for the purpose of creating fear. We were certainly apprehensive, but too busy to be fearful. Commands began ringing out. "Rapid Fire on Fox 1!" We fired hundreds of mortar rounds in support of the company, but we were not able to directly observe the results of our action.

But we were very effective. Lieutenant Charles Petrie of Baker Company later recalled that on one occasion, as dusk approached, 6 Platoon reported that the enemy was forming up in a re-entrant and preparing for an attack. Our battalion of 81mm mortars opened fire on this force and decimated it.

The next two days and nights went by in a blur. We frequently fired large volleys of mortar bombs in support of the rifle companies, and in particular Baker and Dog. After trying and failing to dislodge Baker Company, the Chinese attacked Dog Company in large numbers. Lieutenant Mike Levy, the commander of Dog Company's 12 Platoon, initiated a mortar and artillery bombardment of his own position in order to stem the Chinese assaults. But eventually, we were told that we were surrounded and to expect an assault on our position at any time. Our stress level greatly increased. Would we be able to survive these assaults? We checked our weapons and improved our fortifications.

That attack came in the evening of April 24. We did not immediately notice their presence, but about five hundred Chinese began to climb from the valley floor towards our location. They were advancing quietly in our direction and they were not signalling their approach with bugles and loud shouts as was their habit.

Lieutenant Hub Gray, our 2IC (second in command), quickly took command of the eight .50-caliber machine guns that were mounted on our half-tracks. Whether by a stroke of genius, or as a result of sheer luck, these vehicles were located in a very favourable position for the purpose of confronting the advancing enemy. The machine guns were mounted on circular swivels and could be turned rapidly to any direction. Gray waited until the leading formation of Chinese was only about forty metres short of our position before giving the command to fire. The eight .50-caliber machine guns opened up and began cutting a bloody swath in the Communist ranks.

I was totally unaware of the approaching enemy until the moment that Gray opened fire. We were doing defensive fire tasks for the rifle companies, but as soon as we became aware of the Chinese in our vicinity, we turned our mortars around about 180 degrees, raised them up to an almost perpendicular angle, and began launching bombs on a rapid-fire basis. Our mortar bombs travelled only about one hundred to two hundred metres and began landing in the midst of the Chinese.

It was a devastating slaughter, and by morning we were almost completely out of mortar bombs. The rifle companies were down to a few rounds of ammunition. Our food and water were nearly gone. We were in a desperate situation, but for some reason the Chinese did not continue with their attack, although the trails and roads leading to and from Hill 677 still appeared to be occupied by the enemy. Lieutenant Colonel Stone radioed for help, and soon enough, several Flying Boxcars of the United States Air Force suddenly roared over our position, and parachutes of various colours opened up and drifted into our position. I eagerly helped to open up the canisters and discovered that we had been supplied with mortar bombs, rifle and machine gun ammunition, C rations, and water. A minor miracle had taken place. Robbie Roberts and I piled our fresh supply of bombs next to our mortar. We were ready for action once more.

But everything remained strangely silent. We were not called upon to fire again that day. The next morning, April 26, we were ordered to reload our half-tracks in preparation for a move from Hill 677.

Our descent down was full of tension. We did not know if the Chinese were still present. But nothing happened and we reached the main road in the river valley, where a regimental combat team of the U.S. Army had arrived to take our place. As we drove southward, a powerful feeling of relief surged through my mind and body. In spite of very difficult circumstances, we had somehow survived.

According to Lieutenant Hub Gray, 2 PPCLI lost ten men, and thirty-five more were wounded at Kapyong. We were lucky compared to other UN forces. On Hill 504, three of the American tank commanders had been killed, and the Australians lost thirty-three men, with fifty-eight more wounded. But the Chinese sustained heavy losses too and were not able to break through our line at Kapyong and capture Seoul.

I remained in Korea until the fall of 1951 and then returned to Canada. Although the Battle of Kapyong took place more than half a century ago, I still vividly remember my involvement as a nineteen-year-old private. I have a recurring dream that I am returning to Korea, that the Communists have invaded once again. I am excited but not afraid because I know that I am going to survive and return home.

I still feel a strong attachment to my regiment. Even after many years, the PPCLI is something like a family to me. "Once a Patricia, Always a Patricia."

Private Michael Czuboka (Ret) joined the army in 1950 and served in the Korean War, where his battalion, 2 PPCLI, received the U.S. Presidential Citation for "extraordinary heroism at Kapyong, Korea." When he returned, he trained as a paratrooper and completed forty-five jumps in two years. After leaving the army, Michael went on to become a pilot, a teacher, a principal, and a superintendent of schools. He has taught at the University of Manitoba and in Ukraine, and is the founding president of the Korean War Veterans Association in Manitoba. In his seventieth year, he completed a five-hundred-kilometre solo canoe trip on the Assiniboine River from Brandon to Winnipeg in fourteen days. Michael has published six books, including the Canadian bestseller *Ukrainian Canadian, Eh?* He lives in Winnipeg, Manitoba.

Robbie Roberts and me with an 81mm mortar in Korea, 1951.

This is one of the half-tracks we used in the mortar platoon. The .50-caliber machine gun is mounted on top. In the background is a thatched Korean house.

This portrait was taken in 1952 after I returned to Canada. I was twenty years old and had just qualified as a parachutist, as you can see from the wings on my jacket.

Life Onboard HMCS *Cayuga*

Leading Seaman Leonard Wells (Ret)

We were young and rambunctious, which made a
big difference. I don't know if we were brave, but
we thought we were smart. We thought we were
invincible.

I grew up on a farm in Rapid City, Manitoba, and when I was seventeen and a half years old, I remember reading the local paper with a friend of mine one day, and we saw a big ad that said, "Join the Navy!" He turned to me and said, "Why don't you join, Len?" I had a mediocre job grading eggs at the time, so I quit and enlisted. The egg company folded shortly after that, so I knew I had made the right decision.

I signed up on May 22, 1948. You're supposed to be eighteen to join, but I was tall, and back then, they didn't rely too much on anything else. Funny thing is that my friend didn't join with me.

I signed up in Winnipeg at HMCS Chippawa, then was shipped to HMCS Naden in Esquimalt, British Columbia, where I did fourteen weeks of new-entry training. After I passed and was deemed an ordinary seaman, I was posted to a Canadian cruiser, the HMCS *Ontario*, and we sailed for Hawaii. I was seasick the first three days, but then I got my sea legs and was fine.

Within my first year, I travelled down the Panama Canal to Cuba and back to Esquimalt. I was an ordinary seaman, but I made some friends in communications and would help their office by running messages, and I was learning to type too. They saw my initiative and convinced me to become a communicator, which I did. I went to Halifax for nine months of training: Morse code, flags, etc. And then I shipped back to HMCS Naden for a spell, then posted to the HMCS *Ontario* again. We did some more touring, up to Alaska and some places up north. I had never travelled anywhere before joining the navy. It was so exciting to see the world. Everything was brand new.

On June 25, 1950, the North Korean Army invaded South Korea, quickly advancing over the 38th parallel, pushing southward with such force that the UN stepped in almost immediately. WWII was still in the recent past, and of all Canada's three armed services, it was only the navy that was in a position to help immediately. Three destroyers, HMCS *Cayuga*, HMCS *Athabaskan*, and HMCS *Sioux*, had been preparing for a trip to Europe, so they were half-ready for deployment. The navy called for volunteers, and I stepped forward. I remember being excited. Everything was a big adventure. None of us were afraid we would get into any trouble.

Within two or three days, with my kit bag in hand, I was transferred to the *Cayuga*, a Tribal-class destroyer named after one of Canada's First Nations. We set sail on July 5, just over a week after I volunteered. Our first stop was Pearl Harbor, Hawaii, where we saw a large freighter coming into port, flying funeral flags. We found out that this was a U.S. Navy ship carrying up to ten thousand American servicemen's bodies being repatriated to U.S. soil for burial. This process had been going on in the Pacific Theatre since the end of WWII. Needless to say, the sight gave us some sobering thoughts about what probably lay ahead of us in Korea. From Hawaii, we sailed west to Kwajalein, an atoll in the Marshall Islands, then on to Guam. On July 30, we landed in Sasebo, Japan, just across the Korea Strait from South Korea.

The day after we arrived, we were given our first mission: escort a U.S. ship with UN reinforcements across the Korea Strait to Pusan (now Busan), a southeast port in South Korea. At that time, Pusan was surrounded by attacking North Korean soldiers who were about to push the UN and South Korean forces into the sea. That's when we got nervous because we knew we were getting close to the action, but we completed the escort without encountering any trouble.

A few days later, we were dispatched with a British frigate to destroy all the warehousing and port facilities in the city of Yŏsu, just southwest of Pusan. With our four-inch guns, we blew up everything on the dockyard and then we tackled the jetty. These two hours were the first action of any Canadian ship since WWII.

Meanwhile, back at Pusan, a large-scale battle erupted between the UN and North Korea: the Battle of the Pusan Perimeter. This conflict raged on for six weeks and weakened the hold of the North Koreans. But to turn the tide, we needed to do something bigger. General Douglas MacArthur, heading up the UN effort, decided to launch a surprise attack a long way from Pusan. We were going to Inchon (now Incheon), northwest of Pusan, far, far, far behind enemy lines.

On September 13, the *Cayuga*, along with the *Athabaskan*, the *Sioux*, and a number of other destroyers, began patrolling five miles offshore while heavy cruisers patrolled five miles behind us and the battleship USS *Missouri* lurked another five miles behind them. At dawn, we began the bombardment of the port and island of Wolmido, just a kilometre away from Inchon.

I was the signalman, so I was always on the bridge, reading and sending messages back and forth with other ships, using lamps, flags, and our fifteen-to-twenty-mile-range PVS (passive vision sight). I was one set of the eyes and ears on our vessel. During bombardments, the bridge was very loud, and no one in the navy had ear protection at that time. Our B-gun was just below me, maybe fifteen feet, and the A-gun was forward of that. And we had another four-inch C battery on the tail end of the ship. When they fired off all six four-inch shells, the ship would heave back and forth and we would brace ourselves to remain standing. Overhead, we could hear the two-thousand-pound projectiles from the *Missouri's* nine eighteen-inch guns whoosh by.

After two days of bombardment, hundreds of landing craft sped inshore, unloading marines and army personnel. There was little enemy resistance, and the UN forces quickly pushed inland to reclaim Seoul, the capital. Once they did, all the North Koreans south of the 38th parallel surrendered, a huge coup for the UN, who continued to advance north. The Battle of Inchon proved to be instrumental in reversing the war, and I was excited that we three Royal Canadian Navy destroyers were a part of a big operation like that.

After that introduction to the Korean War, everything fell into a general routine of patrolling, guarding aircraft carriers, and providing gunfire support for the inland guerrilla forces.

It was my duty to be up on the bridge with the officer of the watch and a couple of seamen working as lookouts. If we were in a three- or four-ship group, we did a lot of signalling by lamp so that enemy ships couldn't see us. We would sometimes use our short-range PVS for manoeuvres. We did have a radio room, which we'd use to send messages back to Canada, always in Morse code, but we were mostly low-tech compared to nowadays. When we escorted aircraft carriers, there was a lot of communication needed because planes were either in the air or landing on the carriers. We did most of our signalling for this with flags. To send a message, we'd run three or four flags up to a yardarm; the messages could be "turn ninety degrees starboard" or "turn ninety degrees port" or "increase speed."

We'd escort aircraft carriers for two or three weeks, and when we did, I was usually four hours on, four hours off. If there was a plane landing or taking off, one of the destroyers in the convoy, sometimes the *Cayuga*, would come in just behind the stern of the carrier as plane guard. If it crashed over the side into the water, we would go and pick up the pilot. Later the carriers used helicopters, but during the Korean War it was pickup ships.

Other times, we were sailing around, maintaining the ship and making sure all the ammunition was ready and handy. When we supported guerillas, our seamen were manning guns. And I'd be running back and forth with messages sent between ships.

Quite often, we would be the plane guard. We would patrol a certain area adjacent to the land because we could see these dogfights off in the distance. When our fighter pilots got hit inland of Korea, they would head for the water because they knew if they could get to the water, we would be there to pick them up.

We fell quickly into this routine, with little worry for other dangers, but that all changed on October 16.

That day we were patrolling north of Inchon with the HMS *Kenya*, a British cruiser, when our sonar operator got a ping. He shouted, "I've got mines dead ahead!"

The *Kenya* was some six hundred yards behind us, so I immediately signalled to them with a signal lamp to make a hard turn to starboard. But we were already in the minefield. We had to swing slowly and try to get out unscathed. Our sonar operator had spotted them all over the place, but some areas were a bit more concentrated. We were in the middle of our turn when we heard something scraping along the hull of the ship. A mine.

All these mines were about four hundred pounds of TNT each and had little prongs sticking out of them, and we knew that if one of those hit the ship, it would detonate the mine and our ship would break in half.

We waited anxiously for a minute or two—seemed like an hour—for the explosion to occur, but it never did. The prong must have been defective. We didn't blow up that day, but I'll never forget the sound of that scraping as we proceeded out of the area.

There was no rhyme or reason to the placement of the minefields. The North Koreans and the Chinese, who entered the war in October, would dump them wherever they thought they might hit something. Some were anchored to the bottom of the sea, some just floating. The rogue floating mines were the truly dangerous ones because there was no pattern to them. When we did see them, we would sink them or detonate them by shooting at them with our Bofors guns or rifles. When they blew up, they really exploded. We destroyed a few that way.

———

In November, we were ordered to Hong Kong with the *Athabaskan* for some rest and relaxation, but on our second day out from Korea, we ran into Typhoon Clara, and she was raging, blowing one hundred and some knots. I was on the bridge when I saw a seaman from the *Athabaskan* get swept overboard by a great wall of water that engulfed the entire front section of the ship.

The *Cayuga* swung around to make the pickup and we tried to throw our life jackets to him, but the wind just picked them up and blew them all over the place. Salt water, fortunately, is very buoyant, so it kept him floating even in the thirty- to forty-foot-high waves. Meanwhile, the *Athabaskan* made a turn, swung around, and came right at him.

Two brave sailors went out in the forecastle of the ship, which was plunging up and down in the storm, getting buried in water. They lashed themselves to the guardrail, and when the ship slid alongside the man, a wave crested, bringing him level and within inches of the upper deck. In that instant, the two sailors grabbed their comrade and hauled him on board. It was a miracle. An absolute miracle.

I heard later that he couldn't swim, which was actually quite common for a lot of the men in the navy at the time. Apparently, once he was safe and dry back on board the *Athabascan*, he said, "You know, there is a God."

Everyone was ordered below deck to weather out the rest of the storm as we continued to proceed to Hong Kong. Around 2 a.m., we were sleeping in our mess deck and we began to feel the ship teeter wildly to portside. A rogue wave had hit us on the starboard side with such force that we were going to turn over. The helmsman swung the wheel hard to starboard in an effort to avoid a rollover. Everything began flying about, and we scrambled up the hatch as we pulled on our life jackets. The ship went over fifty-two degrees, which is almost the point at which she would have flipped over and we would have all drowned, but she sat there for a long, long minute and then began creeping back. She righted herself and we carried on, in heavy seas and high winds.

We made it to Hong Kong in one piece, but we soon saw that all the guardrails were pretty well smashed and flattened. The force of the waves had even pushed in some of the guns and heavy armour. We'd been in rough waters before, but never a typhoon that serious. We'd heard of some American ships being lost in typhoons because they were top-heavy, so I was glad that the *Cayuga* had been built right in Canada's own Halifax shipyard.

———

In 1951, I deployed once again for Korea on the HMCS *Cayuga*, and in September, we were dispatched to patrol North Korea near the Yalu

River, which separates North Korea from China. Basically, we were snooping around. Our superiors said they needed someone to go to an island off the coast of Korea along the way, an island quite a bit behind enemy lines. As the signalman, I volunteered, and so did another guy by the name of Peterson. They dropped us off on this island in a small boat. We didn't know if it was occupied or not, but we were instructed to climb to a high point and count the number of enemy ships going back and forth between the mainland and the different islands.

It was a distant island compared to the others that were closer to the mainland, but they were all quite high. Summiting the top felt like climbing a mountain. And it was hot. The whole time Peterson and I were trying to hide ourselves, afraid that the entire place was occupied by North Koreans. I'll never forget, I had a couple of sandwiches and some water from mess, a portable radio transmitter, and one .38-caliber revolver with five shells. Peterson had a Lee-Enfield 303 rifle and five rounds. What were we going to do with those?

We tried to hide behind little shrubs and rocks. I set the radio up ready to call if we got into big trouble, but it would have taken the *Cayuga* one or two hours to get back to us. We just kept thinking what our next move would be if a couple of North Koreans popped out from behind a rock. Fortunately, we did not see any enemy troops, but we did record the movement of a few junks travelling up the coast. Chinese junks are big boats made entirely out of wood, even the sails too. They are actually quite remarkable vessels. They are about thirty to forty feet long and twenty feet wide, and they use the wind to propel them.

We stayed put for about eight or nine hours, until the *Cayuga* radioed me with "We're coming around the corner." They picked us up, and we went back out on patrol as if nothing had happened.

We were frequently patrolling a place called the Amgak Peninsula about halfway up North Korea, where the Taedong River meets the Yellow Sea. We would pull in and set our cutters (small boats) down, and take provisions to the South Koreans that were on a little island close by.

In late October 1951, we were on our usual patrol and had just pulled into the gap and dropped our anchor when the Chinese zeroed in on us. Two shells landed about twenty-five feet on each side of the quarterdeck, spouting water and drenching the men on deck there. Within seconds of the first attack, another shell hit the water some fifty feet off the port bow, followed by two more twenty-five feet off the starboard side. The Chinese had straddled our ship! Instead of raising the anchor, the shipwright hammered a coupling free and the ship's engines thrust into full reverse. Tethered to us were the two motor cutters that we were using to resupply the South Koreans, but they were crushed as we moved out.

We hadn't retreated twenty feet when another shell hit right where we had been moments before. The careening water doused the forecastle and bridge, soaking us to the bone. We just kept reversing. We made a smokescreen with black smoke from our diesel engines, and the captain ordered us signalmen to call the aircraft carriers, out about fifty miles, to send planes in and bomb the hill where the guns were. They responded immediately, coming in with napalm bombs and setting the hill on fire.

We thought that would be the end of our problems in Amgak, but the next day, we came back to get our anchor and they began shooting at us again. We discovered that they had dug a cave back into the mountain and put their artillery guns on rails. They would run them out to the edge of the cliff and shoot at us, then haul the guns back in. We never could get them.

———

When we weren't patrolling, guarding the aircraft carriers, or bombarding coastal ports, life onboard the *Cayuga* was very quiet. We'd play cards and write letters home if we could hold the table down. We kept ourselves busy. We washed all of our clothes. That was the life we picked. We were young and rambunctious, which made a big difference. I don't know if we were brave, but we thought we were smart. We thought we were invincible.

I left the navy on May 22, 1953, after my five-year contract was up. They tried to convince me to re-enlist, to go to officer's school, but I was in love.

I met Marcella in Strathclair, Manitoba, when I was home on leave from my second tour in 1952. She was from Shoal Lake, about twelve miles away, but had come to Strathclair for a square dance, and that's where I saw her for the first time. Her partner never showed and she picked me out to dance with that night. My leave was short, so three days later, I asked her to marry me. And she said yes. It was love at first sight.

Marcella and I got married on July 10, 1954. We have two kids and four grandchildren.

Leading Seaman Leonard Wells (Ret) was born in Rapid City, Manitoba, and joined the Royal Canadian Navy in 1948. He served two tours in the Korean War as a leading seaman CVI (Communications First Class). He received five medals: the Canadian Korea Medal, the Ambassador for Peace Medal (60th Anniversary of the Armistice of the Korean War), the Canadian Volunteer Service Medal for Korea, the United Nations Service Medal (Korea), and the Special Medal from the U.S. 7th Fleet for Military Service, for Gunfire Support. He lives with his wife, Marcella, in Scarborough, Ontario. They have been married for over sixty years.

Here I am in uniform in 1949.

This was taken on the deck of the *Cayuga*. Pusan, where we escorted a ship of UN reinforcements in early September 1950, is in the distance.

On the bridge of the *Cayuga*.

Horsing around beside the Bofors
gun we used to detonate floating
mines or shoot down aircraft.

Marcella and me on our wedding day, July 10, 1954, in Saskatoon, Saskatchewan.

THE VIETNAM WAR

Trapped in Vietnam, 1973

CAPTAIN MORT LIGHTSTONE (RET)

I had gone from playing with my kids in the snow to flying halfway around the world to the middle of war-torn Vietnam. I was in violation of a hard-gained international treaty, with no food, no accommodations, and worst of all, no one to turn to for help.

I was one of six children. During the depression years of the early 1930s my parents struggled to make a living, and for most of my childhood I experienced poverty. I had three older brothers, so my clothing consisted of hand-me-downs. When I learned I would receive a new uniform, new boots and shirts from the air cadets, I joined. I was thirteen and had never had new boots before. How could I have suspected that I was beginning a lifetime full of adventure, intrigue, and some secrecy?

When I graduated from high school, my family needed my financial help and they expected me to find a job. This meant the end of my formal education. My dream of university was put on hold.

It was 1951. The air force was expanding due to the Korean War, which had been raging on for a year. A university degree was a prerequisite for becoming an officer, and the only exception to this rule was to volunteer to be aircrew, otherwise known as "the sharp end of the business." As an aircrew officer, I would have a larger income and be able to provide my parents with more financial support. So, without reluctance, I volunteered for aircrew training. From that day on, I never looked back.

When I graduated from the Royal Canadian Air Force, I was given a five-year commission and I was assigned to 436 Transport Squadron at CFB Trenton in Ontario. Initially, I was trained as a global celestial navigator, which meant I could navigate proficiently by the stars and other heavenly bodies to any location in the world. At Trenton, we were equipped with the giant C-130 Hercules aircraft. We were Canada's global-response squadron. We were trained to fly anywhere in the world at a moment's notice. Often I would go to work in the morning not knowing what continent I'd go to bed on that night. I loved it—it was an exciting life. I described it as "man's work amongst men."

And in 1973, I was about to embark on one of my most challenging missions.

In the 1960s, the U.S. began sending thousands of troops to Vietnam to help the South Vietnamese combat the Communist northern Viet Cong (VC), who were bent on taking over the entire country. This was at the height of the Cold War between the U.S. and the Soviet Union, and the Vietnam War was constantly in the news. We were hearing about hundreds, even thousands, of U.S. troops being killed or wounded each week.

On May 10, 1968, both sides of the Vietnam War met in Paris to discuss the conditions of a ceasefire under the International Control Commission (ICC). By the time an agreement was made, the International Commission of Control and Supervision (ICCS) had replaced the ICC to oversee the withdrawal of troops, release of prisoners of war, and dismantlement of military armaments. It was decided that Canada, Indonesia, Hungary, and Poland—two Communist and two non-Communist countries—would each send two hundred soldiers to Vietnam to implement the terms of the ceasefire. These countries were to be unbiased, impartial, self-contained, and completely independent of any of the armed forces in Vietnam. If Canada needed a paper clip, but that item wasn't written into the Paris Peace Accords, no one in Vietnam could give them one. In the meantime, negotiations dragged on . . . and on. Henry Kissinger, the fifty-sixth U.S. secretary of state, shuttled back and forth endlessly. Weeks became months. Months became years.

At the 436 Transport Squadron, we were told that as soon as the Paris Peace Accords were signed, one of our C-130 Hercules would be dispatched to Vietnam with some top secret "stuff" on board—mostly electronics and communications equipment—and a "Jimmy" from the signal corps. The central figure of the Canadian Signal Corps cap badge is the Roman god Mercury, symbolic of speed, but he is affectionately known to signal personnel throughout the world as "Jimmy."

The date of this mission was a moving target because of the now famous shuttle diplomacy. No one could designate a specific plane or crew members because we didn't know if this mission would be leaving in 1971, 1972, or 1973. Basically, the crew that would be sent to Vietnam would be whoever was available in Trenton when the Paris Peace Accords were signed.

Saturday, January 27, 1973, was a beautiful winter's day. I was home with my kids and we were looking forward to a day of playing in the snow. We had frozen cobs of corn from the summer and were planning a corn roast for dinner. At 9 a.m., I received a displeasing phone call from my squadron. I wouldn't be spending the day with my children after all. I was heading to Vietnam—a combat zone I saw in the headlines every day. Four hours later a quickly assembled crew and I were airborne in our C-130 (E model) Hercules, tail number 130327.

Our orders were to drop off the communications equipment in Tan Son Nhut, a U.S. air base in southern Vietnam. As approved in the Paris Peace Accords, the U.S. forces would refuel our C-130 Hercules, and we were to leave Vietnam within four hours. This was an in-and-out mission.

The most direct route from Trenton to Tan Son Nhut goes right over the North Pole, down through Russia and North Vietnam. There was no way that the Soviet Union or the VC would let us fly over their country. We had to take a more circular route. Trenton to Vancouver, across the north Pacific, stopping at Shemya in the Aleutian Islands, then on to Japan and finally Tan Son Nhut. We put on two crews so that on landing, one crew completed their shift and the other would be fresh to take off and fly the next leg.

The Viet Cong were not happy that Canada was part of the ICCS (sometimes referred to as the "truce team"). As a participant in the Paris Peace Accords, the VC knew every detail of our mission. They decided to give Canada a punch in the nose and intended to destroy our C-130 Hercules. Shortly after the appointed hour of our arrival, a VC commando squad was able to gain access to Tan Son Nhut Air Base through tunnels. They cautiously placed explosives around the parked Hercules and blew the cockpit off the plane.

What the VC failed to realize was that, because of our circular route to Vietnam, we crossed the International Date Line and thus lost a day—*local time*. We arrived the next day! They destroyed some other nation's C-130 Hercules! Almost 95 percent of the wreckage had been cleared by the time we landed, but over the next few days we saw photos that had been taken right after the blast. Clearly, the Viet Cong did not have their hearts in the ceasefire.

The Paris Peace Accords were signed on a Saturday. The next issue

(Monday) of the U.S. Armed Forces newspaper, the *Stars and Stripes*, presented a blazing headline one and a half inches high using a narrow black font: IT'S ALL OVER. Farther down on the same page, another headline about a quarter of an inch high in a similar font read: TRUCE HOUR ARRIVES, ATTACKS RAGING. During the first hours of the Paris Peace Accords, the Viet Cong conducted fear-provoking infractions to the conditions set forth in the accords. The ICCS had disputes and infractions to resolve from the get-go.

When we arrived in Tan Son Nhut, we received a startling secret message from National Defence Headquarters in Ottawa. As I understood it, its essence was that NDHQ were no longer in control of our crew and aircraft—the prime minister and his cabinet were. As I recall the sequence of events, within minutes we were ordered by Ottawa not to leave Vietnam until further notice, but after four hours on the ground we would be in violation of the Paris Peace Accords! We were also ordered to get out of uniform and wear civvies so that the Communist countries in the ICCS would not count 215 Canadians when only 200 were authorized. Yes, from the very start, the Communists were counting heads!

We were now in harm's way, which in the military meant: Be careful *now*, you are very likely to be injured or killed—imminently!

We went to U.S. Colonel Glenn Jones, Military Airlift Command, squadron commander at Tan Son Nhut. In other words, he was the base operations officer. He was busy implementing the terms of the Paris Peace Accords and the retreat and repatriation of the U.S. forces. He was saving hundreds, if not thousands, of lives.

We asked him for help, for food and accommodations, but he tersely reminded us that the accords provided for JP-4 refueling only. He repeated that his hands were tied. After we left, our aircraft commander, Major Dave Watson, pulled me aside and said he had noticed that when we were talking with Colonel Jones, the colonel was extremely terse with everyone except me. He thought that Colonel Jones was more amicable towards me and asked me to talk to him on my own. So I did.

Colonel Jones was very polite, but said he couldn't change his position. The eyes of the world were on him, the ICCS, Tan Son Nhut, and all of Vietnam. His thirty-year career was on the line.

I was upset. During the last few days I had gone from playing with my kids in the snow to flying halfway around the world to the middle of war-torn Vietnam. I was in violation of a hard-gained international treaty, with no food, no accommodations, and worst of all, no one to turn to for help. The Viet Cong were now and then popping out of tunnels to fire at targets of opportunity, and we could hear mortar fire nearby and actions by the guns of the air defences. I was angry, frustrated, and I lost it. I said things to Colonel Jones that I should not have.

Jones unceremoniously threw me out of his office, but before I reached the door he calmed down and told me to come back in an hour. When I returned, he provided me with a box with twenty-four sandwiches and drink boxes and two boxes of cornflakes. I didn't know what we were going to do with the cereal, but I was thankful that he saw to help us.

Colonel Jones told me about an abandoned cell block. It was part of the old French fort at Tan Son Nhut—now a dilapidated and shabby area of the base. Many South Vietnamese civilians working for the U.S. forces lived there with their families. They even had their own taxi company on the base so that their families could go into town for school or to the doctor.

The French fort was in a very rundown area. Within it we found the abandoned cell block, just as Jones had said. It was disgusting. The only way we were going to survive this was to keep our sense of humour. We would joke that, at least, we had running water—the water ran from one corner to the other.

The first few days, some of the South Vietnamese civilians came into the cell block. They were using it as a makeshift laundry. We'd be in the washroom and they would walk in and brazenly do their laundry.

We had other interesting encounters too. The U.S. forces had a ban on bringing any kinds of weapons back to the States, but this war had already been under way for some years, and everybody wanted to bring home souvenirs. They were hoping the rules would change by the time it was their turn to be shipped home. But of course the rules never changed, and many would leave whatever they had acquired to the next GI who got their bunk. I remember chatting with an American airman who was going home in two days. He offered me two thousand carbine rifles. Who knows where he had stashed them away. So much goes on unofficially in a war zone.

Over the next few days, I met with Colonel Jones frequently, and he kept providing me with food as we continued to wait for further orders from Ottawa. He was helping us at a terrible risk to his military career. We didn't speak much during these encounters. I was anxious to stay away from the hangar line and preferred to blend in among the South Vietnamese. Meanwhile, Major Dave Watson was running back and forth between our cell block and Base Operations hoping to find new orders from the prime minister and his cabinet to leave Vietnam.

Our aircraft was equipped with VHF radio transmitters, but these were useless for long ranges, so Major Watson relied on Tan Son Nhut Base Operations for communications. But we were not on an official military communications loop. Rumours were rampant and widespread. We felt completely abandoned in the chaos around us.

Would the Paris Peace Accords hold? Would the ICCS be allowed to implement those accords *peacefully*? We knew the VC were violating the accords throughout South Vietnam. Would Canada withdraw from the ICCS? What if our two hundred Canadians were attacked by the Viet Cong? If they were, logically, our aircraft would be their first escape option.

We acknowledged we had a responsibility as this situation was evolving, or rather deteriorating, and hatched an escape plan.

In the C-130 Hercules we used canvas seating for passengers. People sat shoulder to shoulder facing the next row—knee to knee with the individuals opposite. There were four rows of seats "athwart ship"—along the length of the cabin. Typically the C-130 Hercules could accommodate one hundred passengers. Given the dangers that we were facing in Vietnam, we would never be able to complete two trips, so we had to double our passenger capacity and evacuate all two hundred Canadians in one flight. We knew we could carry the weight—we were used to transporting military tanks—we just didn't have the seats. The loadmasters determined we would install ropes and chains across the width of the cabin, waist high and just a bit more than two feet apart. We would tie the passengers standing to these ropes and chains for the duration of the flight. Of course, we knew that on takeoff everyone would tumble and lose their balance, and probably never regain their footing until after landing—but they would be alive. Luckily, we never had to implement that plan.

We were in Tan Son Nhut for a week when the orders came from Ottawa to immediately deploy to Bangkok. We didn't have to be told twice. We packed in less than three minutes and dashed to Base Operations to get a weather briefing before takeoff. Our Jimmy abandoned the communications equipment after confirming that someone in the ICCS had explosives. If they had to evacuate, they would blow up the secret equipment.

At Base Ops I wanted to say goodbye to Colonel Glenn Jones. Inopportunity had him out of the office blowing up ammunition or some such thing. On the weatherman's desk was a yellow foolscap pad. I wrote a quick note to Colonel Jones thanking him for his hospitality. I come from the school where, when someone treats you nicely, you say thank you with a little gift. What could I give Colonel Jones? I took my navigator's wings off my uniform and at the bottom of the note I asked him to accept my wings as a token of my appreciation. Then we left.

Life changed immediately. In Bangkok, our government advised the Canadian embassy to meet us and do everything they could to make our lives pleasant. They gave us each $3,000 U.S. and a case of whisky, and told us if we wanted more of either, just ask.

We were driven to the New Nana Hotel, 4, Nana Tai Alley, Khlong Toei, which is still in existence. But at that time, the New Nana Hotel was the centre of espionage in the Far East. We were shocked to see lieutenant colonels from many nations of the world having drinks or dinner together, spilling confidential information that their governments had ordered them to leak.

We went from sleeping on the floor of that cell block to each member of the crew having his own immaculate air-conditioned room in the New Nana. We stayed there for just under three weeks, waiting to dash back into Tan Son Nhut and pluck out two hundred Canadians, but it never happened! Those dedicated and principled two hundred Canadian soldiers remained in Vietnam for six months, until on July 31, 1973, Canada pulled out of the ICCS. During that half year there were over seventeen thousand infractions of the Paris Peace Accords recorded and seventy-two thousand people killed or wounded.

I went on to do a lot of other exciting things in the Canadian Air Force. As a world-class navigator I flew vast distances north, south, east, and west. I've traversed the world several times and met challenges presented by the aurora borealis in the Arctic, blowing sandstorms in the Sahara, the pressure pattern winds of the Atlantic, and the *reverse* Coriolis effect south of the equator, and survived a 6.2 earthquake in the heart of the Pacific. In addition to participating in three significant wars, I was involved in numerous mercy missions for the United Nations around the globe. I retired from the air force with

6,600 hours flying on military operations and missions. I have been a proud member of an Officers' Mess for more than sixty-five years.

Late in December 2013, I received a special letter from Jones. As I opened the letter, my eyes fell on the letterhead. I gave a slight gasp when I saw the words "Major General." I thought, *Good for Glenn.* I started reading the first line. "Today I was looking through a folder of papers that belonged to my father." When I read those words, I realized immediately that Glenn was gone. My eyes darted back to the letterhead, and I saw that this letter was from a Major General Duane Jones, Glenn's son. Duane's letter to me repeats word for word what I wrote on the yellow note to his father. A little while later Duane scanned the original note and sent it to me.

Colonel Glenn Jones enjoyed nineteen years in retirement. His son had joined the U.S. Air Force, become a major general, and retired. A long passage of time, and yet, reading that note, I thought, *Wasn't it just last week I was in Vietnam?*

Captain Mort Lightstone (Ret) was born in 1932 and joined the RCAF in 1951. Subsequent to his twenty-eight years of military service, he was a senior manager with the CIBC. He has received commendations from the Canadian minister of veterans affairs and the U.K. Aircrew Association. He is a Memory Project ambassador and a volunteer workshop leader for chronically ill individuals. Mort lives in Toronto, Ontario.

RIGHT: Here I am in uniform in the 1950s. I would later give the wings on my chest to Colonel Glenn Jones.

BELOW: The crew of 436 Transport Squadron hurriedly assembled at CFB Trenton in front of our C-130 Hercules. Our Jimmy is kneeling on the far left, and beside him is Major Dave Watson, our aircraft commander. I'm standing behind them, third from the left.

27 Dec 2013

CAPT Mort Lightstone
3300 Don Mills Road
Toronto, ON M2J 4X7

Dear Mort,

Today I was looking through a folder of papers that belonged to my Father. He was a United States Air Force officer who retired in 1974 after 31 years active service. During the Viet Nam war he served as the Military Airlift Command squadron commander at Tan Son Nhut. So, back to those papers...

I found a hand-written note on a sheet of yellow legal tablet. The note said:

Dear Glenn,

CAF 6848 is away this A.M. And I would like to thank you for your hospitality while we had our short stay at Tan Son Nhut. Please accept the enclosed Canadian Armed Forces Navigators wings as a small token out our appreciation.

It is my thought that a peace will never come as a result of fear of war but rather only as a result of a love of peace.

Good luck

Signed
Mort Lighthouse, Capt

That note means a lot to me and I believe you are the man who gave it to my Father. Thank you for your kindness and your humanity. Seems to me that time has validated your perspective.

God Bless You,

Duane A. Jones

I received this letter from Colonel Jones's son just a few years ago. Subsequently, the major general sent me a copy of my original note to his dad.

Dear Glenn,

CAF 6848 is away this A.M. and I would like to thank you for your hospitality while we had our short stay at Tan Son Nhut. Please accept the enclosed Canadian Armed Forces Navigators wings as a small token of our appreciation.

It is my thought that peace will never come as a result of fear of war but rather only as a result of a love of peace.

Good luck

Mort Lightstone Capt.

89

THE HOME
FRONT

HMCS *Montreal*, Atlantic Ocean, 1998

LEADING SEAMAN RON CLEROUX (RET)

*It started with a pipe—a command over the ship's
broadcast system. I was aboard the HMCS Montreal
and we were patrolling the eastern coast near Halifax
when a distress signal came in to one of our rescue
centres. The SOS came from just off the coast of Saint-
Pierre and Miquelon around five o'clock. It was such
a faint signal that they lost it immediately, a solid
indication that something severe had happened.*

My story wasn't in the headlines. It wasn't in a war in a far-off land. Most people think of the Swissair 111 crash when I tell them I was involved in a bad search-and-rescue mission off the east coast of Canada, but it wasn't that. This is my story.

From a young age, I was always fascinated by the military. I used to read all the military books my dad had around the house. My great-uncle served in WWII, and my cousin achieved the rank of chief petty officer of the Canadian Armed Forces, the highest rank for a noncommissioned member. By the time I was a teenager, I knew I wanted to be a part of my family's legacy. In 1989, I was seventeen and still too young to join without my parents signing off, so I asked my mom to sign the papers. She did, and I reported to the recruiting office the next day and asked to join the navy.

I trained as a marine engineering technician, and my job was to run and operate the ship. In the old days, we marine engineering techs were called stokers because to make the engine go, we had to stoke the fire, throw coal into the boilers, and produce steam. Now it's done by the push of a button, but we still use the term "stoker."

On the ship, everyone had different duties, besides our trades. When we were getting supplies, I would be a line handler. In emergencies, if you weren't on watch, you performed different duties from your usual ones. In case of an attack or a fire onboard, I would be part of one of the ship's fire teams and would stand by and await fire, flood, or casualties. In addition, I was trained as one of the ship's team divers, so if anyone fell overboard, I could rescue them. For rescue stations, I would act as the rescue diver or the RHIB (rigid-hulled inflatable boat) stoker. We would also regularly inspect our hulls for any needed maintenance and search for mines which might have been placed by other divers. We constantly practiced these drills. The navy is part of the Standing Naval Force Atlantic, a rapid-response force, and we were always on the ready. We were always working, always in uniform, because we needed to react at any given moment.

In 1998, I'd been in the navy for about nine years, served in one NATO mission in 1995, and I knew I'd found my calling. We were constantly travelling from port to port, visiting new places all over the world and meeting new people. But on January 16, 1998, all of that was about to change.

It started with a pipe—a command over the ship's broadcast system. I was aboard the HMCS *Montreal* and we were patrolling the eastern coast near Halifax when a distress signal came in to one of our rescue centres. The SOS came from just off the coast of Saint-Pierre and Miquelon around five o'clock. It was such a faint signal that they lost it immediately, a solid indication that something severe had happened.

We went full speed to an area close to the signal point where we would meet the Canadian Coast Guard vessel (CCGV) *W.G. George*, a fifteen-by-five-metre Arun-class lifeboat that had also been dispatched.

As the *Montreal* neared our meeting point, we went to our rescue stations even though we wouldn't know the full situation until we were on the scene. The CCGV had already arrived and begun recovering casualties. Our executive officer (EO) directed me and my buddy Mike, another ship's team diver, to make contact with the CCGV and assist with the removal of the bodies on their deck as well as any bodies in the water. Along with Mike and our boat coxswain, Joe, I got into the 7- by 2.75-metre RHIB and we were lowered into the darkness below us.

We hadn't noticed the pitch of the seas when we were aboard the *Montreal*, but now in the little RHIB, the pitch of the ocean could make any hardened sailor queasy. The hard stench of diesel fuel was inescapable.

When we reached the CCGV, they told us they couldn't recover any more bodies. The fuel oil from the ocean had soaked their deck, making it near impossible to operate the vessel in the rocky waters. But there were more bodies to recover.

We began to realize that this wasn't a rescue mission.

With the help of the CCGV's spotlight, we located a casualty bobbing in the turbulent waves.

"What do we do?" Mike asked.

I laughed, my first defense against fear. "How am I supposed to know?"

We'd trained for this so many times, but the reality of what we were witnessing was sinking in. It was surreal.

We asked Joe to slow down so we could recover the body. It was soaked in oil, and as I reached for the life jacket, it ripped in my hands.

The ocean was so choppy we realized we needed the protection of the side of the *Montreal*. We held the body in the water until we got closer to the ship, then hauled it into the RHIB.

We screamed up to the *Montreal* to take the body, then dispatched to the awaiting CCGV. Again, they used their spotlight to locate more casualties in the water. And again, we lugged the bodies into our RHIB and brought them back to the *Montreal* with great difficulty.

The CCGV needed to transfer the bodies they had recovered to us, but the ocean was still rolling and we couldn't tie the two ships together without risk of capsizing or rolling inwards to the other vessel. As a solution, we planned to hold on to the two ships. I would be the anchor, and should the rolling get extreme, I would let go and we would drift off.

I sat on the RHIB engine bonnet and held a stanchion of the CCGV while they lowered the bodies down to us. Under those conditions, we all had to move quickly, so this was hasty work. One casualty landed in my lap and I started gagging. Everything was just too real. Mike could see me struggling and yelled for me to get it together, that we were almost done. I managed to hold on until we got back to the *Montreal*.

I knew I needed to get off the RHIB as soon as possible, but we were stuck down in the crashing waves because the ship was concerned that with all the extra weight, the RHIB was too heavy for the cable. We screamed back and forth until they lowered a Billy Pugh, a collapsible transfer device. Mike jumped in the Billy Pugh, not using the proper techniques. He was supposed to grasp the netting on the outside and stand on the rigid ring on the bottom, but he jumped in the middle of the Billy Pugh instead. I think he wanted off as soon as possible as well. They lowered the lines down to us to attach the RHIB on the bow and stern so to keep us steady, then they lowered the steel clasp and cable to haul up the RHIB, and we were brought to deck level.

Once on deck, I stripped off my wet-weather suit, which was soaked in fuel oil and death, and ran below. I heard the coxswain ask me if I was all right. I wasn't, but I couldn't let him see that. It was dark and the ship was illuminated with the red lights we used at night. He couldn't see my tears.

Below deck, I broke down pretty hard. I couldn't believe what we'd just done. I stripped down completely, threw my clothes in a bag, and showered, but I couldn't scrub the smell of diesel off me.

I went to the mess for a drink to try to drown out the faces I'd seen in the water. The mess president came in to see if I was okay. I kept my head bent, hiding my tears, lied and said I was fine. He grabbed me another dozen beers, gave me a pat on the shoulder, and went off to bed. I stayed and polished off the beer.

I later learned the details of the *Flare*'s demise. The ship had set out from the Netherlands for Montreal, but had been caught in a vicious storm that cracked the vessel in half. The weather had escalated so quickly that the crew didn't have time to dispatch all the life rafts, and those who did get aboard them weren't properly dressed in their immersion suits. Within thirty minutes of the ship's break, the stern sank, polluting the water with fuel oil. Twenty-one of the crew perished, and four survived.

After that recovery mission, life became hard. I was very angry and I started drinking more than I ever had before. I would black out and wake up with flashes of memories from the night before. I'd remember picking fights with friends. Then there were nights when I locked myself in the bedroom and curled up in a ball. I gave up on a lot of things I loved: my kids, sports, coaching, work. I was a marine engineer, and yet I couldn't stand the smell of diesel fuel. I would get dizzy, nauseated, and anxious.

That summer I deployed on another NATO mission. We joined the remainder of the NATO task force in Mayport, Florida, but ended up leaving hastily because of an impending hurricane.

But I knew something was wrong with me. I tried to reach out, in a non-direct way, but I couldn't get out what I was feeling inside, what I was going through. I started to feel sorry for myself, and any ache or pain became an excuse. I stopped exercising and quickly gained weight. I thought I hurt before, but now I was lugging around so much extra weight.

In 1999, I broke my ankle. After surgery and recovery, I started exercising again, playing rugby. I began feeling good about myself once more. I wanted to get back to the ship, but I knew I needed help to do that. Despite the physical exercise, I still saw those faces in the dark. I would leave rugby practices early and head to the gym to avoid any conflict. Sometimes I would have an outburst and get angry at the coach or other players. Believe it or not, rugby is a sport where you actually need to have a cool head. I was useless. I would work out hard and get a good sweat on so no one would notice the tears that would inevitably come.

I asked my EO if I could do the Nijmegen March, an annual four-day march in the Netherlands that promotes sport and exercise. I thought maybe if I could do something like that, it would help in the healing. He wasn't aware that I was struggling with PTSD, and because I had taken time off to recover from my ankle injury, I was told no. Again, I was angry. Since I was seventeen, this life was all I'd known, and I loved it. The military was everything to me, but now we were at odds.

I begrudgingly went to the Medical Inspection Room (MIR). Those five minutes I spent talking about my feelings were the hardest moments of my life. The doctor diagnosed me with PTSD and helped me get into the Occupational Trauma and Stress Support Clinic, which was just being developed at the time to help those dealing with trauma.

That was the beginning of my healing process. I was assessed and began regular therapy. Even now, whether I need to talk or need to understand how to handle a situation, my therapist is there to help me. I learned how to open up, to be a civilian. After so long in the military, that wasn't such an easy thing to do.

For further assistance, I used programs offered by a variety of veterans' organizations that were geared to helping military guys like me. I hiked the Rockies with Outward Bound and travelled to the North Pole with True Patriot Love. In 2016, I received a road bike from Soldier On. I had no previous road cycling experience, as I had always used a hybrid bike to commute everywhere in the city. The road bike allowed me to participate in the 2016 Invictus Games, initiated by HRH Prince Harry, who created the games to allow those like me to show others that the power of sport could be used to recover, to generate a better understanding in the general public of what we had been through, and to foster respect for wounded, injured, and sick veterans and servicepeople.

My experience with the Invictus Games was interesting to say the least. Team Canada had two camps prior to leaving for Orlando. The first was a meet-and-greet, and to choose which sports we wanted to compete in. I fully engaged myself with this task. If people were going to be watching us, I wanted to put on my best performance. I trained twice a day, six days a week. I developed a schedule. As an ex-military person, I thrive on timing, so going to the camps, while nice, threw me off my schedule a bit. But meeting my teammates and not having to cook were positives. I ate five to six times a day to keep my energy levels up. I still do. There is always a piece of fruit at hand, a protein bar, or a meal in the fridge ready to go.

After months of training on my own it was time to head to Florida, but before we left, we met up in Toronto to enjoy a baseball game and relax. This is where I started to feel all the anxiety. I tried to do what I normally would, but ended up sabotaging myself. I went out for *a* drink the last night. And I almost didn't make it on the bus the next day. If it hadn't been for my roommate, Duane, and the team doc, I think the management would have left me at the hotel.

Invictus flew our guests to Florida. My wife, Nickie, and my youngest daughter, Chloe, joined me for this adventure. I learned from other athletes and their spouses that Invictus wasn't just stressful for me. We all dealt with it in different ways. Nickie was mine and I was so glad to have her there. She knew exactly what to say, how to calm me down, relax me. Invictus took care of our families so nicely. No matter where we went, everyone was smiling and saying hello to us. I was so empowered by these events. Watching others with visible and non-visible injuries made me realize life wasn't so bad. That I could move on and keep up a healthy lifestyle.

I competed in the field events shot put and discus, the road cycling time trial, the road cycling criteria (or crit as they say in the cycling world), and two indoor rowing events. I won the bronze medal in the four-minute row and silver in the one-minute row. That's when I knew I was back.

Today, if I had the chance to join the navy again, I would do it in a heartbeat. Nothing beats the brotherhood, being a part of the military family. I've experienced a lot more good than bad, and that bad will never cloud how I see the military. Honour, pride, and service are what we're all about. It was a rocky road to get where I am today, but I'm here and I wouldn't change a thing.

Leading Seaman Ron Cleroux (Ret) joined the Royal Canadian Navy in 1989 and served for sixteen years. He served aboard HMCS *Saguenay*, a DDH (destroyer, helicopter carrying) destroyer in Halifax, Nova Scotia, at the age of eighteen, and did tours on the *Skeena* and *Terra Nova* before being posted to HMCS *Vancouver*, a Canadian Patrol frigate, in 1990. He served on HMCS *Montreal*, twice, before and after completing his Qualifying Level 5 to become a marine engineering technician. Ron received a Special Service Medal and Canadian Forces Decoration during the 2000 Tall Ship sail. He won two medals in the 2016 Invictus Games. Ron lives in Halifax, Nova Scotia, with his family.

A candid shot taken during basic training at Cornwallis in 1989.

Here I am training for the 2016 Invictus Games.

Receiving the Bronze Medal for four-minute indoor rowing was a big victory for me.

The Morgue in Hangar B, CFB Shearwater

Major Trevor Jain, MD

*They gave me a medical brassard (red cross) to put
on my arm, then a driver drove me up to Hangar B.
I didn't know then that I would be spending twelve to
sixteen hours a day in Hangar B for weeks to come.*

Second Lieutenant Jain!" Warrant Officer Parker shouted.

"Warrant!" I replied.

"You're in the breach. Orders in ten minutes."

It was summer 1990, the last week of my platoon commander's course at Camp Aldershot, my home base in the West Nova Scotia Regiment, and I was about to act as the platoon commander for the next mission. We had started with thirty candidates and were down to fifteen and I was exhausted, going on sheer willpower, but since I was a West Novie, there was no way I was going to be RTU (returned to unit) without a passing grade. The directing staff were circling like sharks just looking for a reason to send home reservists, or "part-time soldiers," like me.

Just three years earlier, at seventeen, I had joined the army as a rifleman. The army had been offering an eight-week youth employment program with no further commitment required after completion. I needed the money for tuition and for flying lessons—at that time I was aiming to be a professional pilot. I didn't know anything about the army when I joined, but I loved being in it. Where else could I get paid to be picked up by Huey helicopter, march 10 km with a rucksack, throw a grenade, do a quick attack, and make my 0830 stats class at Acadia University?

Back in the breach, I received my orders—conduct a deliberate attack on a fortified position—and started my battle procedure: seventeen steps to accomplish any mission given to a soldier by the army. I carefully did my map recce, issued my own initial warning orders, and planned how to wield the firepower of an infantry platoon. I wanted to go big and ensure mission success, so I decided to take all three support weapons: the 60mm mortar, the Carl G (a rocket launcher), and the C6 (a medium machine gun). My battle plan was solid, the mission was a success, and I became a qualified platoon commander in the historic West Nova Scotia Regiment. It was the proudest day of my life.

Over the next two years, I continued to work in the military and, in my spare time, received my pilot's license, but the biology program at Acadia had gotten me interested in medicine. I wanted to gain more exposure, so I began volunteering at the Valley Regional Hospital in Kentville, Nova Scotia.

I was volunteering in the pathology lab one day when the chief pathologist, Dr. Roland Jung, stopped me in the hall.

"Hey, Trevor, you still interested in learning how to do an autopsy?"

I nodded enthusiastically. I had asked a month earlier if I could observe an autopsy, thinking it would be a good way to get hands-on knowledge of disease processes and anatomy. And I had a good relationship with Dr. Jung. He was very interested in the military and had nicknamed me "Bison commander" because the summer before

I commanded a fleet of thirty brand new Bison armoured vehicles at the Combat Training Centre in Gagetown.

As we walked down to the morgue, Dr. Jung explained the purpose of autopsies and the processes, methods, materials, and workings of a morgue. I nodded along, but I must confess, I was a bit nervous. I had never seen a dead body before.

One of the first things I noticed was the smell, but it didn't seem to affect Dr. Jung. With the utmost professionalism and care, he began the autopsy and was quickly able to delineate and confirm why the patient had died just a few hours before. After completing the autopsy, he demonstrated how to close the body up in preparation for transfer to the funeral home. In everything he did I saw the immense amount of respect he had for the patient in front of him. That was when I knew without a doubt that I wanted to pursue medicine. Between my classes at Acadia and my reserve unit, I volunteered as much as possible with the pathology lab and eventually went from observing to assisting with autopsies and human-remain logistics. Little did I know how useful this knowledge, my infantry training, and even my flight experience would become.

———

On September 2, 1998, I decided to try to go to bed early. I was still part-time in the military, working out of the 36th Canadian Brigade Group (CBG) HQ in Halifax, had just entered my fourth year of medical school, and was starting my psychiatry rotation at the Nova Scotia Psychiatric Hospital. After hitting the books for a few hours, I went to bed, and my brain was swirling with the DSM-IV criteria of bipolar, depression, and anxiety, and my own wonderings about what the following weeks would bring.

I woke up to my phone ringing. I looked at the clock—0315 hours. Why would anyone be calling me so late?

I picked up the phone. "Hello?"

"Trev, it's Rick." I had met Captain Rick Dykens at the West Novies, and he was the operations officer at 36th CBG.

"Yeah, listen, turn on your news. There has been a plane crash and I need you at Shearwater."

I knew Rick to be a prankster and this was before Twitter and Facebook, so my first thought was that maybe he was out and about on the west coast for a military conference and was pulling my leg by calling me in the middle of the night. I hung up on him.

At 0330 hours, the phone rang again.

"Rick, I got class tomorrow early . . ."

"Trevor, it's not a joke. We have a major plane crash. I need you at Shearwater ASAP. Report to the base clinic when you arrive. I'll get you a drive."

"Roger." I wiped the sleep out of my eyes and stumbled to find my uniform, my heart pounding. A plane crash? Why Base Shearwater? I hadn't had a lot of experience with trauma and Rick hadn't given me any details about casualties. Only later did I find out he anticipated a request for assistance from the provincial government, and had set up the ops centre at brigade headquarters and issued warning orders to the four infantry battalions in Nova Scotia.

I had just finished dressing when I heard a knock on my door. It was a RCMP officer. "I'm your driver," he said. "Let's go."

With lights flashing, he took me from Halifax to Shearwater in record time. I asked him what was going on, but all he knew was that an MD-11 airliner had crashed off the coast of Peggy's Cove and that they were searching for survivors. I knew that this was a big transatlantic plane from when I would see them at the Halifax International Airport, where I flew my own plane. The number of casualties could be greater than two hundred. When we arrived at Shearwater, the base was locked down and there were military police (MPs) everywhere. I showed my ID to get through the gate and then an officer brought me to the clinic. "Good luck," he said.

My mind was racing. Inside the clinic, I ran into a medical officer. When I said my name was Trevor, he asked if I was "the guy with pathology experience."

I nodded, and they gave me a medical brassard (red cross) to put on my arm, then a driver drove me up to Hangar B. I didn't know then that I would be spending twelve to sixteen hours a day in Hangar B for weeks to come.

The hangar was loud, chaotic, and confusing. Aircrew were sitting around talking while other civilians and soldiers were running around in circles. Yellow tape marks covered the floor, and I realized that they were indicators for the bodies. No one could tell me who was in charge, but I heard someone mumble that it was Dr. John Butt, the chief medical examiner for Nova Scotia.

I recognized a flight surgeon sitting with some aircrew, and I asked him if he could give me a situation report. He indicated that he and some other health care providers were flown up from Greenwood expecting an influx of casualties, but he was told there were no survivors, so they were heading back. Just then, a frustrated truck driver entered the hangar and asked if anyone knew how to get the portable X-ray machine off his truck. I did, so I volunteered to "drive" it off. When I went to park it in the corner of the hangar, I saw long black hair trailing out from under the tarp. All at once, I was transported back to my first autopsy. I felt shocked and nervous but determined.

An EMO (Emergency Measures Organization) carpenter came to me and asked if I was the guy with pathology experience and told me that Dr. Butt had sent word back from the crash site to start building a morgue. I asked for notebook and a pen and sketched out the requirements to build twelve- by twelve-foot suites, then started a list of supplies that would be needed to conduct autopsies, multiplying everything by ten. Hangar B was basically a large, empty warehouse-like room, but the team there demonstrated keen initiative and solved any problems on the fly. They took my drawing and worked with EMO plumbers and electricians to build Suites A and B with hot water, electricity, and drainage.

When Dr. Butt arrived, his administrative assistant, Linda, who was one of the people who knew what was going on, told him that I had significant pathology and military experience and was also a pilot. He asked if I was responsible for getting things somewhat organized. I said yes, and he replied, "Sounds good. Get my morgue up and running."

Then he called everyone to meet in the hangar and told us that Swissair 111, a large airliner, had crashed off the coast of Peggy's Cove and that everyone was presumed dead. This was no longer a rescue mission, but a pathology operation in conjunction with the Transportation Safety Board of Canada investigation.

After the meeting, I phoned the dean of medicine at Dalhousie University to tell her what I was up to. She was amazing and told me that she would look after my rotation while I focused on my military assignment.

Using the battle procedure I had learned in the infantry, I tackled my mission. Immediately, I began putting together pathology teams, each with a pathologist, a medical examiner RN, an RCMP scribe, and a roving DNA technician, so we could begin identifying victims. With the RCMP, we quickly designed an ad hoc protocol for handling the remains. They came up with a cataloguing system for the property and body parts that we would encounter, and I started a stores list and asked our base liaison for rations and quarters for the members working on the autopsies. The first team in Suite B was set. The time was 1030 hours on September 3, 1998, approximately twelve hours after the crash.

We got the first body bag from the refrigerator truck. It was a heavy-duty dark-green bag with black handles. I asked the team if they were ready and we opened it. The sight and smell were like nothing I had experienced: a mix of JP-4 fuel, sea water, decomposing water-soaked flesh, and traumatized body parts. It was a nightmare. The photographer for digital records said, "Oh my good God." The faces around me turned white and pale, some broke out into a sweat, and one person vomited. All I could say was "These poor people."

After what seemed like an eternity of stunned silence, I slowly started to dictate what I was seeing. "Male hand with gold wedding band on left fourth finger. Traumatically amputated from wrist." I asked for Neil, our DNA tech, to come to the suite, as I was able to get a muscle tissue sample, and DNA was required for definitive identification. Any personal items were catalogued and removed to a different room.

We kept a record of each body part. And there were so many in the bag. The smell started to become overwhelming, so I suggested we put Vicks VapoRub under our noses. I would end up ordering crates of this.

At one point, I looked up to see a half dozen CISs (critical incident stress counselors) watching us work. I stopped my team and had the CISs leave the morgue. Post-traumatic stress disorder was not talked about in the military, so although the counselors were well intentioned, their presence interfered with the operational chain of command and made it difficult for my team to talk, should they want to.

Ten grueling hours later, we were done with the first bag. I debriefed my team and then Inspector Lee Fraser from the RCMP, Dr. Butt, a member of the Department of Justice, and I met to discuss the obvious problem. If these were the types of remains that we had to identify, our operation was going to take too long. We hashed out a new protocol where we would divide the remains into significant and non-significant body parts, significant parts being those that lent themselves to identification, like fingers, teeth, tattoos, congenital birthmarks, etc. We agreed on how to proceed, and then I was given a key for a room with a shower. Thank God for the air force's provision of quarters and rations. I was exhausted.

The next day during our morning brief, Dr. Butt read from a book about letters to God from children. In the packed room, all we could hear was his calm voice. This set the tone for the day and put a smile on everyone's face before they entered the morgue to do the unthinkable. He helped us concentrate on the family members who needed the closure identification could bring. He read for us every day until we left.

At 0700 hours I was back at the morgue and reinforcements had arrived. Without Sergeant Art Davis from the Medical Branch, a man not easily rattled, and the reserve medics from Sydney and Halifax, the morgue would not have functioned. When two dental trucks with X-ray showed up, we drove the vehicles right into the hangar. We could start making IDs.

I verbally led Team A through the new protocol and went next door to Suite B, where my team was ready. The next body bag was brought in and we began again.

Late in the second day, we opened a body bag to find an almost-intact person. In all the ugliness, we had the chance to do something beautiful. We put in hours of suturing to prepare the body for visible identification. When we were done, she was taken down to the chapel, where her family identified her. This was the only visible identification confirmation that generated a legal death certificate out of the 229 people on board.

Meanwhile, ante-mortem data about the victims was starting to come in from embassies around the world, and our record section was compiling dossiers on each victim that matched ante-mortem data to post-mortem information, helping us identify the victims and confirm the manifest.

That evening, my team was getting ready to get another body bag for identification. When we opened the bag, we saw a distinguishing tattoo covering an entire back. We thought we had an easy identification on our hands, but once we discussed our findings with the ante-mortem data shop, we discovered there were actually two passengers with this same tattoo on board. And they weren't related. This taught us the valuable lesson of not assuming anything while doing these autopsies.

The teams were forming an incredibly strong bond. At the end of each day, instead of rushing home or trying to get to the shack for some shut-eye, we would slowly leave Hangar B. We all had difficulty leaving the workspace as we felt a deep sense of remorse for the families, but knew if we could identify their loved ones, well, at least that was something good in the middle of this tragedy.

By the fourth day, senior leadership dropped by. I briefed Admiral Miller, the JTFA (Joint Task Force Atlantic) commander at the time, on the morgue part of the operation. His EA (executive assistant) gave me his card and told me if I needed anything or ran into issues to "call direct." The next day, a navy supply officer unexpectedly burst into the hangar, wanting to see for herself where all "her supplies" were going. I told her politely that she was in the wrong hangar, that her supplies were being used in Hangar A. It was an unwelcome disruption and I wanted to avoid any more in the future, so I called the EA for Admiral Miller, who informed me it would be looked after. After that, an RCMP officer was posted at the entrance of the morgue.

We continued to work during the day and into the evening. At around 2100 hours, an officer came to our suite and said, "Trevor, some military guy wants to see the morgue and get a briefing." We were not aware of any scheduled visitors and I was gowned up for the work, but I said to let him in. The "military guy" was the Chief of Defence Staff General Maurice Baril. He introduced himself, and I got my latex gloves off as quickly as I could and gave him a brief. He asked whether it was my infantry training or my medical training that was helping me out the most. I replied, "Both, sir!"

Around this time, I began noticing some signs cropping up to bring some levity to the gruesome work we were doing. "Fingerprints

'R' Us" was placed over the suite that did the fingerprints. Someone had added to my location board, "The Doctor is out to lunch." A plastic skeleton appeared with the name "Trevor" written on its forehead and somehow was left where I would go to dictate. Whenever I was dictating, Trevor the skeleton would have to be moved, which invited a few chuckles. When I could, I encouraged humour in this setting. It was a good way to cope.

But then, just when we thought nothing could surprise us, we opened a bag to find the remains of two babies. I stopped the autopsy immediately and got everyone out of the suite, then went back to complete the autopsy on my own. I did not want the team exposed to this type of trauma. One of our initial team members had informed us that he could no longer hold his child since starting these autopsies. What we were doing in Hangar B was beginning to affect everyone.

For the next four weeks, we continued our daily rhythm of morning briefing, autopsies, meals, then sleep. At that time, the army decided to pull me and the reserve medics out and allow civilian organizations to take over running the morgue. On the Friday before we left, Dr. Butt called me to his office and thanked me and the team for the outstanding work we had done. He wished we could stay, but knew we all had our lives to get back to. Then he gave me some cash to take the medics out that night in Halifax.

We had been told in a mandatory group CIS briefing that we should take the next forty-eight hours for quiet reflection and not to go out and consume alcohol, but we disagreed. The medics and I set up an RV point and we hit the town hard that night. It was the best decompression session I ever had.

On the weekend, I took a close friend with me and drove out to Peggy's Cove, the crash site of Swissair 111. We could still see the ships out there recovering people and things. I have never been back since. The rest of the week, I felt extremely alone and was eager to get back to class. I had missed a whole month of school, but fortunately the dean of medicine arranged for those four weeks to count as a medical rotation. She was later recognized for this support with a national award from the Canadian Forces Liaison Council.

Just a few months later, in January, I had to fly across Canada to interview for various residency programs. I could not imagine sitting in an airplane, looking at the upholstery or the backs of passengers' heads. The airline was kind enough to flag my ticket and let me board first and deplane last, avoiding other passengers. They also let me ride in the jump seat for all my flights.

What I saw and did in Hangar B stayed with me. After the crash, when I would shake someone's hand, I would start a mental dictation of what I was seeing. "Caucasian hand, scar noted on fourth finger." Sometimes, I will be walking down the street and all of a sudden get a whiff of airplane fuel for no reason. Even today, the smell of Vicks VapoRub makes me cringe.

In 1999, I decided that I had done enough pathology for a lifetime and entered family medicine, then emergency medicine. I deployed with the military multiple times to different environments, but nothing compares to those tragic weeks in Hangar B where a quiet bunch of reserve medical professionals did the unthinkable with 100 percent mission success. All persons were identified by November 11, 1998.

Major Trevor Jain, MSM, CD, MD, MSc, grew up in the Annapolis Valley in Nova Scotia, where he joined the West Nova Scotia Regiment as a rifleman when he was seventeen. For his efforts during the Swissair 111 disaster, he received the Meritorious Service Medal. He graduated with distinction from Dalhousie University Medical School in 1999, and continued to serve in the military, deploying both overseas and domestically. After briefly leaving the forces to pursue emergency medicine, he reenlisted as the 36 Canadian Brigade group surgeon in 2010 and was cross-appointed as the regimental second in command of the Prince Edward Island Regiment. He completed a master's of disaster medicine from the University of Brussels, where he conducted original research in mass casualty response that was later presented at a NATO medical conference in Paris, France. Trevor recently returned from Operation IMPACT (with the coalition against ISIL). When not attending patients or teaching, he enjoys flying his airplane over the Maritimes. He lives in Prince Edward Island with his wife, Kara, and twin daughters, Sydney and Natasha.

Within six days, the entire morgue in Hangar B was completed. We had eight fully functioning suites and fingerprint, radiology, and dental stations.

This is Suite B, where the first autopsy took place. I worked in this space for four weeks.

RCMP Inspector Lee Fraser and me on day seven of the morgue operations. After our briefing, I would change into my scrubs and get to work.

Basically Broken

Captain Kelly S. Thompson (Ret)

*When my right knee started to ache, I didn't think
too much of it. Most of us were hurting in some form
or another and complained of chaffing that made
our thighs look like ground chuck, blisters the size of
small countries, and other pains.*

If anyone were to inspect my military career—hold it up against the
light of those who deployed, fired their weapons to protect themselves
and others, left their families for months on end—I'd pale in compari-
son, by a lot. For eight years, I was a logistics officer in the Canadian
Forces with a human resources specialty, and my life was spent riding
a desk, pushing papers. My job was horribly, impossibly unsexy.

It's hard not to shrink back in subservience when you come from
generations of war-hardened soldiers, and my family legacy is long
reaching. There's my great-grandfather, a recipient of the British Empire Medal after his service in WWII; my Grandpa Jarvis, who braved
the navy seas during WWII as well; my Grandpa Thompson, a Korean War infantier; and my father, a peacekeeper in the Golan. And
then there's me. The only one to enrol in the air force. The only one to

join as an officer through the Regular Officer Training Plan, where I could earn a university degree at the same time. And of course, there's the stark fact that I am the only female. That last bit, the whole gender issue, felt like something I had to shake off to believe that even though I liked makeup, painted nails, fashion, and art, I could be a good soldier. That was the battle I felt I was fighting.

So although I didn't grow up dreaming of life in the military, what I did want was a connection with the soldiers that came before me. I wanted the camaraderie, the teamwork, the sense of purpose. In hindsight, I probably wanted the essence of military life without all the shit that came along with it, unaware that it was the shit that would teach me the most about myself and others. The shit would highlight my strengths and help me to ignore my weaknesses.

I idolized, probably in too romantic and naïve a sense, the soldiers in my family. I used to carry with me a letter my Grandpa T had received from a friend of his, dated June 19, 1951, thanking my grandfather for saving his life:

Well, Tommy, that is enough of my troubles as what I really wrote for was to thank you and any of the other boys that helped in fixing my wounds and getting me out of there, as I know what a job it was. . . . I want to thank you fellows for all you did for me and some day, even though it seems impossible, I will do something for you. You're top dog by me.

It was signed, "Your Old Sidekick, Art."

I relished phrases like "top dog by me," and "thank you fellows," and other iconic fifties slang, not appreciating the pain between the lines. When I grew older, even then not fully understanding the calamity of such a letter, I kept a photocopy tucked into my journal as if just keeping the paper with me would show I came from a line of bravery. I needed to prove it to myself as much as to anyone else.

Although the military experience was one I never thought I'd have, when the Twin Towers were terrorized, I was in my last year of high school, and with a dad already serving, it suddenly felt like the right thing to do. How do any of us explain those callings that ask us to do something greater than ourselves, even when fear tries to push us in the opposite direction? Me? I shipped off to basic training in Saint-Jean, Quebec. Tucked in my luggage were hairspray and uniforms, lip gloss and shoe polish. I was a walking oxymoron.

It's hard to explain just how useless I felt as a soldier, and this was highlighted by some rather dismal basic training results. Other than an awesome score on the range, it seemed I wasn't cut out for the demands on my body, and I watched with envy as some of my platoon-mates cruised through the challenges like ducks taking to water. Was I the only one who could not do any more push-ups? Was I the only one who fantasized about a world that did not involve several different iterations of obstacle courses?

For those in the ROTP stream, basic training is broken down into two different summers, with the remainder of the year dedicated to university schooling. And the act of obtaining a degree in professional writing did nothing to make those around me (or myself, for that matter) realize my soldier destiny. "What the fuck do you do with that?" they would ask. "Write books?"

But by some miracle of soldier wizardry, I made it to the final week in the field during the second summer of training. Just one week stood between me and military success. So we loaded the buses, packed our rucksacks, and were dropped off in the fields of Farnham, Quebec, for several training exercises.

When my right knee started to ache, I didn't think too much of it. Most of us were hurting in some form or another and complained of chaffing that made our thighs look like ground chuck, blisters the size of small countries, and other pains. But eventually, my knee got so bad that I couldn't take it anymore and asked to go to the MIR, the base hospital, where I limped my way into the clinic in shame. Admitting an injury in the Forces isn't easy—by far my greatest challenge, even in the face of all the physical ones.

But after a physical exam at the MIR, I was dismissed with a handful of ibuprofen. "It's just tendonitis," the medic said, rolling his eyes when I raised my eyebrows in incredulity.

"Are you sure?" I poked and prodded at my knee, the flesh all swollen and angry.

"That's it."

"So what do I do now?"

"Well, you should be on some restricted walking duties, but that isn't likely out in the field. Or you can elect to go back to Saint-Jean if you feel like it's that bad."

Never had I been so tempted by an offer in my entire life. I could go back to Saint-Jean, to my shitty thin mattress in my sweltering room. But then the reality that I would have to return to the field after surviving two entire summers of basic training hit. If I turned back, I was giving up, only to have to repeat the process from the start. Plus, it was just tendonitis. Soldiers before me had dealt with far worse. "No," I said. "I'll stay."

"Well, then get back out there."

Idling in the dusty parking area was a master corporal, who was waiting in a vehicle to take me back to my fellow troops. When I asked what I was supposed to do now, considering the suggestion of walking restrictions, he shrugged his soldiers. "You soldier on, Officer Cadet."

Back with my section, I was ordered to help lace some modular tenting, and I moved quickly, full of assurance. If only my leg had received the memo that this was not the time for giving up. Upon reaching the next section of tenting material, fingers at the ready, my right knee gave way. Out of pain? Exhaustion? A trip on a tree root? Who knows? But when I fell forward and my kneecap clattered to the ground, I couldn't help but cry out sharply, hissing air through my teeth and clutching my knee to my chest in the fetal position.

"Thompson, shit!" shouted my platoon-mate. "Hey, Sergeant!" Everyone came running.

I knew they were hovering over me, but I couldn't open my eyes. Just clutched and rolled back and forth across the ridge of my spine, waiting for the stabbing sensation to subside. When my eyes finally cracked open, the sergeant had his hands on his hips, bottom lip jutting out in annoyance.

"You okay to keep going?" he asked, shading his eyes from the sun.

I thought of Grandpa's letter, now tucked into the secret Velcroed pocket of my uniform, close to my heart. "Yes, Sergeant." I stood. Christ, I still have no idea how I managed to stand, let alone march for another thirty kilometres over the next three days.

Hours later, after dinner, my platoon stumbled along a sandy road plunked in Quebec's backwoods. My moist camouflage uniform was clinging to my skin like I'd been dunked in honey. I knew then that this was more than tendonitis, that I had broken something somewhere in the dusty field while schlepping that seventy-pound rucksack, my C7 rifle slung around my neck and my body crippled with exhaustion.

For our final night in the field, our section was on a mini exercise, the goal of which seemed irrelevant to all of us. March from point A to point B. Set up camp. Shoot at potential, imaginary enemies. We took shelter from the sun until it dipped behind the pine trees, affording the opportunity to rehydrate and change damp socks. I nestled in a ditch with my platoon-mate Joe and gnawed on my contraband beef jerky while my leg throbbed a cadence with my heartbeat. I offered Joe a piece of hardened beef and sensed he understood the importance of this gift. In the field and at war, calories and protein are to soldiers what cocaine is to an addict.

"Well?" Joe said, half-masticated beef rolling under his tongue. "Let's check this bitch out." He gestured towards my leg.

I pulled the fabric sand trap from my combat boot to assess the damage, rolling the camouflage material up to my thigh. My knee looked like it had swallowed a basketball and was covered in a blotchy purple bruise.

"Looks like shit. You sure you can keep going?" he asked.

"Do I have a choice?"

Joe cocked his head sympathetically, his blue eyes catching the last of the sunlight. He appeared to be hardly sweating in the sticky heat, nor did he seem tired or covered in sand flea bites like the rest of us. He didn't even present the standard officer-cadet eye rings from sleep deprivation. Joe was the kind of guy who made basic training seem easy, like one of the models in the recruitment videos where obstacles are leaped over with ease, punctuated by rigid salutes befitting national pride. But it was impossible to hate him for it. It was impossible to hate Joe for anything at all.

I brought my shoulders to my ears. "I've got to 'soldier on,' right?"

Those were the orders from the master corporal earlier. *Time to soldier on*, which meant to keep marching even though I felt my leg threatening to snap like a twig. I chewed my jerky pensively as I leaned against my ruck and stared up at the darkening sky.

"Give me your rucksack. I'll carry it back to camp," Joe said.

"I'm fine. I'll be fine," I said, waving him off. One man, one kit. Another military mantra.

As our platoon packed up, Joe reached out a gentlemanly hand to heave me vertical. Somewhere in the distance, an artillery simulator went off, the sound of mechanical gunfire automatically directing my trigger finger to my rifle's safety switch, my body at the ready. The simulator painted the sky with artificial white light that highlighted our faces hidden in the shadows of the trees. Collectively, we paused, waited. No more gunfire. We could keep moving.

I hefted my bag onto my shoulders and winced as I meandered onto the dirt road. I could barely see the end of the lane, and I knew that I could not, or would not, reach the end no matter where it led.

Joe adjusted his rucksack onto his chest and squatted in front of me.

"Hop on. I'll piggyback you to camp."

"You can't be serious. It's three fucking kilometres! Between me and the bags, that's over two hundred fucking pounds." Swearing is just one of the things that unites us soldiers. Swearing, boot-polishing, and suffering in militaristic solidarity as we choke down another cold individual meal pack.

The whole scenario seemed ridiculous, but so did the idea of hobbling back to camp myself. I shimmied my bag onto the ground, where it landed with a thud, a plume of sand making us cough and sputter. I rested my hands on Joe's broad shoulders, slightly damp from the humidity, and closed my eyes to fight off a wave of pain-induced nausea. He smelled like Tide laundry detergent—a miracle after a sweaty week in the field without a shower.

Once I was on his back, Joe lumbered steadily as a determined tugboat while I clung to him, a broken-down cargo ship. He carried me the entire way, my rucksack dragging in the dust like a mitten attached to a string.

That night I slept under the stars in nothing but a bivy bag, shivering even though I wasn't cold. And then, the next morning it was over. We had passed the course, emerged through to the other side. And yet even on the bus on the way back to the base, I couldn't bring myself to celebrate. When we arrived in Saint-Jean, smelling like garbage and in various states of disrepair, we lay in the sunlight, rucks at our side.

"You're the only injured chick who made it." One of my platoonmates gestured to me with a nod of his head. I was the only one of four injured women who had chosen to stay in the field and not return early, although I'm not sure if I actively made the choice or if the option to forgo the physical madness was ever given to me. The fellow cadet was in his late thirties, a former infantryman who had already been to Afghanistan and was training to become an officer. He seemed out of place in our crowd, the mark of experience and war apparent in his eyes and the solemn way in which he went about his tasks. "That's something to be proud of. You took it like a man."

Like a man. Perhaps I had taken it like a man, whatever that meant. All I needed to do was march thirty kilometres on a leg that turned out to have been broken in order to prove it. Would the respect for completion have been diminished had I pushed my concerns on my course staff? If I had pushed for more testing or a doctor's assessment, would that have made me a "wuss"? A less worthy soldier? At the time, stacked next to my long list of soldier shortcomings, I worried the answer was yes. I rolled up my pant leg again for a cursory inspection now that basic training was over, and both the colour and size of my kneecap drew significant attention.

Once I was home in Toronto, a month later, my suspicions were confirmed, although the exact moment of the break was uncertain. After complaining of increased pain during my assigned physiotherapy, I was sent to a civilian orthopaedic surgeon, who finally ordered an MRI. Apparently it began as a stress fracture, but was damaged further by continued marching while carrying too much weight for my new 135-pound frame. I didn't know it then, but my tibia injury would bring nerve pain as sharp as pins, and, later, pervasive, achy arthritis, all before I was thirty. *You should have stopped marching once it started to hurt*, the civilian doctor said. I laughed at the preposterous idea.

But after our return from the field, for just a moment, I basked in the knowledge that I was a soldier after all. I wondered if Grandpa T would have been proud.

My broken leg led to chronic pain, surgeries, nerve-burning treatments, steroid injections, more surgeries, and even injections of my own bone marrow into my knee joint. Six years later and nothing, it seemed, could fix me, and as much as I had never wanted a military career, I felt immense grief at the idea of leaving the life that had shown me how to hammer out my own mettle, my own worth. I was slated for a medical release in September 2011, without ever having deployed overseas. My injury stopped my career before it ever really started.

My final year in the Forces was spent working at an Integrated Personnel Support Centre dedicated to helping injured and ill soldiers. My coworkers and I used to joke that I was like a guy from that spray-on hair commercial: "I'm the president, and a client too!" As an injured soldier myself, my career coming to an end, I tried to commiserate with the troops who came in, most of them Afghanistan veterans, their injuries more hidden than my own pronounced limp.

My greatest service to the military (and it's an admittedly small list), was that one special year at the IPSC. Most of my workdays, I sat and listened to the soldiers who shut my office door and shared their agony, anxiety, and depression from their wartime experiences. They always spoke in anxious whispers, as though the idea of pain was something unbefitting a soldier. Other than the acts of war themselves, being vulnerable—voicing those aches out loud—is the most difficult task that can be asked of a soldier.

"You're allowed to hurt here," I would say, my standard line. "No shame." Then I would listen. Sometimes for hours. Occasionally, I would take them to lunch so they could keep talking. I was not a trained counsellor. In fact, I hardly ever spoke. But I listened. To those soldiers, wherever you are: I heard you. Your stories stay with me every day.

There's a part of me that hates that when I broke my leg in the field, I had to be saved by my platoon-mate and friend Joe Shorrocks. I wanted to do the saving, at least of myself, but accepting that help also brought me an incomparable connection with the man who would, ten years later, become my husband. Joe held my hand after I signed the release papers and became Kelly Thompson, not Captain Thompson, and didn't let go as depression and grief over the loss of military life took hold. As I had with all those soldiers who came through my office at the IPSC, he understood that the act of listening was all I needed to feel understood by someone else who had lived the military life too.

As I scrabbled my way out of depression, I decided the best path was to return to my passion for writing and to pursue a graduate degree.

The night before my first day of school, I studied the University of British Columbia campus maps. Planned where I would park. Noted all nearby restaurants easily accessed by foot. And in the morning, I woke up early to get ready, pack a lunch, make a coffee for my new travel mug. I did everything but make an operation order to conduct my mission of a successful first day of my master's degree.

I remember rambling to a military buddy on the phone. *How am I going to go back to school, after all these years? I mean, am I even any good at this writing thing?* My friend didn't allay my fears. "What the hell are you going to do with a degree in creative writing?" he said, stressing the words *creative writing*, as though they didn't belong in the dictionary. I didn't have an answer for him.

As part of my course, I was assigned the task of writing a twenty-page essay, which my classmates would critique and I would read aloud. My essay was about my first military funeral and I knew it wasn't very good. For years I'd been shaping and honing this piece, trying to give life to all those squashed emotions on the page. And I'd staked my whole ability as a writer on those few precious pages.

I'd never done a public reading before, and the faculty was composed of literary legends, lending to my stress. As I got to the podium, my hands began to shake and my heart raced, and I swore the entire room could hear it throb into the microphone. I tugged my crumpled pages from my pocket and took two deep breaths. My practise giving lectures in the Forces had not sufficiently prepared me to share something so personal and gritty.

"Perhaps it was naïve of me, but I had hoped to avoid any brushes with death while I served in the Forces, but Afghanistan robbed me of this hope . . ." I was at the part of the essay where I visited the Movements Unit in Quebec, the tour ending with a glimpse of the refrigerated military caskets used for transporting fallen soldiers from overseas. Reflecting on that moment as I read from the page, the sacrifice of the troops who had travelled in those coffins felt as tangible as the audience in front of me. I looked up from the page and my peers were captive. Their eyes said, *Keep going.* I started the next sentence, but heaving breaths were ragged in my throat and my words became unintelligible; through sobs, I managed to blurt out the rest of my story before flopping into an audience seat, spent and shaking. My less than heroic performance horrified me into silence for the rest of the night while I listened to my fellow students in an eerie haze. When the lights flashed on, I collected my purse and made for the door.

"Excuse me." A woman tapped me on the shoulder and I turned to find Susan Musgrave, wildly famous Canadian Poet Extraordinaire. "That was really beautiful. You've got some stories to share, and those stories are important. Keep writing."

I said nothing as she walked away, unaware of her impact, the heat of her hand still burning on my skin. I returned home to find Joe already in bed reading a book.

"How'd it go?"

I leaned over to give him a kiss, a smirk tugging at my lips. "I think I'm finally where I'm supposed to be."

Later, I lay in bed unable to sleep, plot ideas and poetry lines rattling about in my head. I tiptoed into my office and pulled out my fabric-covered journal, left untouched since my military release. When was the last time I had used a pen and paper? My hand hovered over the page, hesitant, began a few lines then scratched them out. Doodled toy soldiers then scratched those out too. My feelings rolled around at the end of my tongue, uncertain.

I found my tribe.

Few of us are so lucky as to find a place where we belong. For a long time, I worried that my writerly nature and penchant for lipstick made me a military outcast, and sometimes it did. And then when I became a civilian, I worried that a lack of literary know-how was a stain on my creative résumé. Too artsy for one side, too military for the other, I was convinced that these two passions of mine could never mix. But I now know that this straddling of borders is what makes me unique, both in the military and outside of it.

I still limp. I have pain every single day. I'm often asked, if given the choice, would I go back in time, stick to my artistic guns, and forge a writing career, forgoing the military experience that would give me a permanent disability. These people are often surprised when the answer is an absolute, unequivocal *No*.

There are so many positives to my military career that I have a hard time listing them all. I made extraordinary friends, found a husband I cherish, and had some truly unique experiences. What I learned over almost a decade of service was that the challenge of basic training and then the further challenge of such a life-altering injury led me to a greater understanding of myself. I arrived in Saint-Jean with the assurance that I was too girly to do anything worthwhile, and then I picked at that scab as I continued to settle near the bottom of the professional pack. It was only after I broke my leg that I learned how committed I was to the experience and how far I would push if it meant I could be a part of an organization that helped others live free and safe lives.

So was I a great soldier? I'm not sure. Am I a great writer? Jury is out. But what I am is grateful, for friends, for the military, for my own determination and strength, and for all the other soldiers who wondered about their own abilities but still found it within themselves to search for an answer to the question.

Captain Kelly S. Thompson (Ret) joined the military in 2003 and served eight years. In 2014, she graduated from the University of British Columbia with her master's in creative writing. Kelly's writing has appeared in *Chatelaine, Embedded on the Home Front: Where Military and Civilian Lives Converge* by Heritage House Press, *Boobs: Women Explore What It Means to Have Breasts* by Caitlin Press, and more. She won the 2013 Barbara Novak Award for Personal Essay, and her fiction won the House of Anansi Press Golden Anniversary Award. She lives with her husband and dog, Pot Roast, in whichever location the military settles them.

ABOVE: Joe and me sporting naïve smiles and our ID discs on the final day of our first summer of basic training in 2003. We'd be married more than a decade later. I keep this photo tacked up above my writing desk.

LEFT: My final military photo, taken by my dad just before I handed in my kit on retirement. I'm doing my best to look like a soldier.

PEACEKEEPING

My Best and Worst Days Flying with the RCAF

MASTER WARRANT OFFICER
WILLIAM MUNDEN (RET)

Immediately we saw from our window the Voodoo jet
arc over in flames and splash into the ocean. Then,
out from the cloud came two parachutes.

I was fifteen the first time I went up in a plane. I was working for the summer at a tourist resort just north of Parry Sound. I would clean people's fish, stock their wood stoves with wood and kindling, and refuel their boats with gas. One day, a fellow flew in with a single-engine Seabee aircraft to take anyone who wanted on a ride. I had never flown before and was pretty apprehensive about it, but there was nobody around but me, so I thought, *I'll spend five dollars for a fifteen-minute ride with this guy.*

We took off from the water, and at about seven hundred feet, the engine quit. Without breaking into a sweat, the pilot turned the plane around, glided back down, touched down on the water, and cruised right up and nudged the beach where we started from. I thought, *Hey, there's not much to this flying.* From then on, I was always interested in airplanes.

Two years later, I joined the air force. I was seventeen and had to have my parents' written permission to join. I was sent to the Manning Depot at Saint-Jean, Quebec, and learned to go left, right, left, right, yes sir, no sir, and all that. I was also given aptitude tests and was selected for training as an aero engine technician. Then I went to Camp Borden, the birthplace of the RCAF, for six months of engine training.

My first operational posting was in Winnipeg, and I worked on C-47 aircraft (the military version of the DC3), which I thought were pretty neat. Shortly after that I started flying on them as a technical crewman. The C-47 really required quite a bit of tender love and care between flights, so I would service it whenever we landed. I would put on the wing and engine covers, refuel, and do the after-flight maintenance, making sure that there was always lots of fuel and oil. Before takeoff the next morning, I'd spend a couple of hours preheating the engines, taking the covers off, and running the engines.

I really enjoyed flying and got to fly all over Canada, including many flights to Arctic territories. When I was on leave, I would come home to Toronto in my uniform. That's when I fell in love with Nancy.

We had lived just three blocks apart growing up and had gone to public school together, but we didn't date or even acknowledge each other very much until after I joined the air force. She says it was the uniform that did it. We started dating on October 5, 1956—our first date was a football game—and we got married two years later. For our honeymoon, we drove back to Winnipeg together.

I spent about ten and a half years in Winnipeg and was qualified on three different types of aircrafts, including the Albatross Flying Boat, which was used for search and rescue. In 1967, the Albatross was moved to the RCAF station at Comox on Vancouver Island, and I thought, *Wow, I'd like to go there because the weather is a lot nicer*. It became my centennial project to snivel my way to Comox with the two Albatrosses, and I was successful.

At the 442 Transport and Rescue Squadron in Comox we had the busiest search-and-rescue area in the country because we were responsible for the entire province of B.C., part of the Northwest Territories, all of the Yukon, and a good deal of the west coast. We were on standby twenty-four hours a day, 365 days a year. When a call came in, we were to be airborne in three minutes. At night, when we were home, we had thirty minutes to get to the airport, get the airplane out of the hangar, and be in the air. The very best and proudest day of my career happened here in Comox.

———

February 18, 1971, was a cold, windy day, and I was scheduled to do a bit of hoist training in our Labrador helicopter, a big, versatile aircraft well suited for search-and-rescue missions. The Labrador had a 135-foot rescue cable that we raised up and down underneath the aircraft to hoist people off a boat if we were over the water or out of trees if we couldn't land. We'd send this cable down and people could hook on to it. If we were over the water, we had a Billy Pugh rescue net, which looked like a big upside-down badminton bird with a floatation collar that we used to scoop up bodies from the water without landing.

That day we took off in the Labrador for a little remote island about eight miles away, to practice our hoisting. We were just off the air force base when a "Voodoo," one of the jet fighters from a different unit on the base, took off down the runway. Instantly, it was over the Strait of Georgia. All of a sudden we heard a very loud *beep beep beep* in our Labrador—the Voodoo's emergency locator transmitter had been activated, indicating that one or both of its crew had ejected.

Immediately we saw from our window the Voodoo arc over in flames and splash into the ocean. Then, out from the cloud came two parachutes.

We found out later that just before the Voodoo went up into the clouds, about twelve hundred feet above the sea, its left engine suffered a catastrophic failure that resulted in a large ball of fire.

Since we were already in the vicinity, we actually had to keep a bit of distance so that our rotors didn't interfere with the two men as they were coming down. When they did hit the water, we saw immediately that one of the crew was completely fine. It was as if he wrote the book on survival: he had his one-man dinghy out, his boots off, and his knife out to cut the shroud lines from his parachute away from him so that it wouldn't drag him around.

The navigator's experience was just the opposite. He had been sitting behind the pilot, and when they blew the canopy—that great big piece of Plexiglas roof over the cockpit of the plane—so they could eject themselves, a ball of fire came right into the cockpit just as he was pulling his lever to eject. The fire was essentially burning jet fuel, and the inhalation incapacitated him. When he hit the water, he wasn't able to release his parachute. It was a very windy day, and the parachute was dragging him along in the cold, rough sea.

We could see that he was having the most difficulty, so we went to him first. We flattened his parachute with our rotor wash—basically, the air from our helicopter was so powerful that the parachute flattened and released—and readied the hoist.

Our hoist stuck out from the side of the aircraft like a boom. We opened the door on the side of the helicopter and attached the Billy Pugh net. The hoist cable went from a big drum inside the aircraft through the open door, around another pulley on the end of the boom, and then straight down. I was operating the hoist that day, so I was in my harness kneeling at the open door, with a switch in one hand for operating the hoist cable, and in the other, a microphone switch to talk to my pilot. My job was not only to raise and lower the hoist but also to direct the pilot whether I wanted him to go forward, left, right, up, down, or steady hover, etc.

I had done only two or three practice water scoops before, with

Annie, our CPR dummy. I had never managed to get Annie on the first pass, and here we were faced with our first live body. This guy had arms and legs—Annie didn't. Once I got the Billy Pugh net down into the water, I told the pilot to go very slowly. We were between fifty and seventy-five feet from the water. We didn't want to get too close because then we would be kicking up too much water with the rotors, and that would make it more difficult to control the Billy Pugh net and the cable hoist. On our first pass over the navigator, I managed to scoop him up. It was the one and only time in my life that I did that, and it was because of extremely good teamwork.

We got the navigator up and into the Labrador. We could see he wasn't very coherent and his whole head looked like it was submerged in a bucket of froth. But we had him and he was alive. Then we just had to move over about four hundred feet and pick up his pilot.

Because we had been going to practice, we had para rescue people on board, and when this incident happened, they started getting into their wetsuits. But before they finished, we had both Voodoo crew on board.

We raced back to the base at quite a bit higher than the allowable airspeed for the Labrador, with our door still wide open. We came screaming in, landed right in front of the hangars, and passed the Voodoo crew off to the waiting ambulance for transfer to the base hospital. Only nine minutes and forty seconds had passed since the Voodoo had taken off.

The next day we went to see the navigator in the hospital, but they wouldn't let us into his room because they didn't want his facial burns to get infected. So we said hello to him from the doorway. He went on to recover fully.

In December of that year, 442 Squadron was having a Christmas party in the Comox Legion. We were a very tight-knit community in search and rescue, especially on the helicopter side. In the middle of the party, in walked the Voodoo navigator. His voice was faltering and he had tears in his eyes, and he said, "I just want to thank you all for saving my life." He put three bottles of Crown Royal on the mantelpiece, turned around, and walked out.

I found out later that he was sent to Vietnam as a member of the Canadian observer corps. I was a flight engineer in 436 Transport Squadron Trenton at that time, flying on Hercules aircraft, and was scheduled to do a supply run to the Canadians in Saigon. I hoped to run into this navigator, but it was a nasty day. There was a lot of heavy shelling going on off one end of the runway in Saigon, so we quickly dumped off our supplies (which included two thousand pounds of Labatt Blue for our troops) and we left. I never saw him again.

But the Voodoo pilot actually lived on the same street as me, Dogwood Avenue, in Comox. At the time of the accident, he was a captain, but he later was promoted to lieutenant colonel and became the commanding officer of 442 Squadron. The same squadron that had saved him!

I had moved on by then, but was back on Vancouver Island, in Victoria, working as an air cadet liaison and was to oversee the graduation parade for the glider school in Princeton, B.C. I found out that the ceremony's reviewing officer was this very pilot, so I called up his secretary and asked if he would sign my logbook. And he did. Under the line "Pilot Recovery from the Voodoo," he wrote: "Thanks, Doug Stewart, Voodoo Pilot, Thirteen and a half years later."

In August 1974, I was with 436 Transport Squadron in Trenton, and every once in a while we were tasked to go to Lahr, Germany, with our Hercules aircraft to move people or equipment around to Canadian installations in Europe. We were called the Lahr slip crew, and we'd stay in Germany for a couple of weeks at a time doing a variety of jobs around Europe and the Middle East.

On August 9, we were listening to Armed Forces Radio in the lounge of our flyers' hotel—really a converted barrack block—when we heard that a peacekeeping aircraft had been shot down near the Golan Heights and the entire crew was lost. I was horrified to hear that an unarmed, peacekeeping transport aircraft doing the same things we were doing had been shot down. We knew there were only Canadian aircraft flying out of Cairo in support of the UN—Buffalo 461—and I personally knew both the pilots in the small detachment. Which one had been flying, or had they both been aboard?

Somehow we knew we were going to be involved in the events that followed, and went to bed anxious, but sure we were going to have a long day ahead of us tomorrow. I guess the wheels were turning all night at the UN headquarters in New York, at the National Defense headquarters in Ottawa, and at the Canadian Forces Europe headquarters in Lahr. Sure enough, we were roused out of bed early the next day with a new task. Go to Damascus, Syria, and recover the remains of the nine Canadians on board.

More details were released to us at that time, including the names of the aircrew aboard the Buffalo 461. My heart sank at the sight of the list—at the top was the name of a friend, Gary Foster, the pilot of Buffalo 461. Gary and I had fished for steelhead trout in the Puntledge River near Comox many times when we were both flying with 442 just a few years earlier. Now I learned that his plane had been blasted out of the sky by not one, not two, but three heat-seeking missiles.

The airway—that electronic highway in the sky—into Damascus had been shut down, so we were ordered to go to Cairo, Egypt, and await UN clearance.

Once in Cairo, we waited for further instructions, but they did not come, so we spent the night at a snazzy hotel called the Mena House. It was situated across the Nile River, on the west side of the city, close to the Pyramids and Sphinx, a beautiful spot, but I did not enjoy being there under the circumstances. The next morning, I walked up the hill to see the Pyramids, trying to get my mind away from what lay ahead, but I was unable to.

By ten-thirty that morning we began getting antsy because we didn't want to fly into Damascus after dark. We were just a big flying transport truck, unarmed just like our fallen friends. Late that afternoon we received news that our clearance was pending. We headed to the airport and readied our Hercules for when the clearance came in. I remember thinking, *If we don't get airborne in the next few minutes, we're not going.*

We decided that we would take off, and hopefully along the way, we'd get our clearance via radio. We weren't happy about that, because radio is not a very secure way to get a clearance of that importance, but we had to rely on the fact that it would be a genuine thing coming from the UN. We weren't allowed to travel over Israeli airspace en route to Syria, so our route was less direct. We went out over the Mediterranean, to Cyprus, made a hard right turn and headed for Beirut, Lebanon. From there it was a sixty-five-mile flight over the Golan Heights into Damascus.

We got to Cyprus in daylight, but by the time we turned and headed towards Beirut and Damascus, it was dark. Then, a most frightful thing happened. On the final circle of our spiraling descent into Damascus, just about over the point where the Buffalo 461 was hit, we turned on the landing lights, and poof! Something white went flying right by the cockpit windows. Everybody had their hearts in their mouths for a second. It was probably a bird, but the adrenaline was surging in us and it almost made us overshoot our landing. However, we gathered our wits and finished the approach and landing.

Things deteriorated on the ground as tensions between officials from both countries were high.

We needed fuel, almost twenty thousand pounds, to get us back to Lahr. Because we were a global operation, we had international credit cards, called Carnet cards, which allowed us to purchase fuel from just about anywhere on earth, except Damascus, we soon found out. The two-bit fuel driver pulled up his truck and told us we needed an Air Total credit card. We had Texaco, Shell, Mobile, Exxon, but we didn't have Air Total, so he wasn't going to pump us any fuel.

I had to go and search out the brass from the Canadian High Commission to remedy the situation, and we finally got an interpreter who talked some sense into the fuel truck driver.

However, this delayed the ceremony. We had to refuel and ready the Hercules to accept the caskets so we could take off as soon as the ceremony ended.

By the time the ceremony started, it was very dark. The airport had just a few lights, and we could see two lines of soldiers standing, waiting for the caskets. A few Syrian soldiers were lined up on one side, and Canadian peacekeeping soldiers from the Golan Heights were lined up on the other side. They began bringing the caskets one at a time through this column of opposing military soldiers.

There has always been a big rivalry throughout my whole career between the air force, the army, and the navy. We were always teasing them about how poorly their systems worked and how well ours did. If we had to take army people somewhere, we'd kid with them that they'd finally found a good way to travel.

Nevertheless, on that night, in Damascus, I was the proudest I'd ever been of those Canadian army peacekeepers. These were the soldiers that went out and picked up the bits and pieces of our fallen comrades in the Golan Heights. They found wooden ammunition boxes and fabricated caskets. They stole some wood-grain "mack tack" and covered the boxes, then put on their best uniforms and stood at attention in that airport while the remains were brought onto the Hercules. I thought, *Boy, how can you do that?*

Just as they were bringing what was supposed to be Gary's casket, I took a couple of pictures on my cheap old camera. It was at night and I couldn't see very well through the tears in my eyes.

Once all the caskets were loaded, we climbed into the Hercules and took another moment or two to try to clear the tears away, to read the checklist and get things started.

When we were ready, we didn't waste any time getting out of Syrian or Lebanese airspace. We didn't really start breathing fully until we were out over the Mediterranean. In those days, we were allowed to make short personal telephone calls through the military high-frequency radios, so over the Mediterranean, we called our base in Trenton and asked them to phone patch us to our homes.

I phoned Nancy. Of course, it was the middle of the night in Ontario. She had heard on the radio that a Canadian air transport plane had been shot down, so she was a bit antsy for a while. We weren't allowed to say much in the way of details because it was an unsecure radio frequency, so I just said, "Hi, we're out over the Mediterranean, headed towards Lahr." She could read between the lines that we were out of Syria.

After a seven-hour, fifteen-minute flight, we rolled to a stop in Lahr around four o'clock in the morning. We handed the remains over to the base medical staff that were charged with safekeeping until our military Boeing 707 departed for Canada later the next morning to bring them home. We were tired and sad. The two pilots and I killed a bottle of wine, had breakfast, then went to bed.

That month, I was way over my flying limit of one hundred hours a month, so the medical officer grounded me and I had to come back to Trenton as a deadheaded passenger. I was completely exhausted.

Our Hercules, number 307, ended up being the highest-flying-time Hercules in the RCAF, and in 2016, they sent it to the museum at the Canada Aviation and Space Museum in Ottawa.

I went on to do many other interesting and exciting missions, but August 9–11, 1974, remains the lowest point of my career. I've always felt that the Buffalo Nine didn't get the attention or respect they deserved, perhaps because President Richard Nixon's impeachment was going on at the same time. The only real thing that our government did was set aside August 9 as Peacekeepers' Day in Canada, but I've found that hardly anybody knows about it. Peacekeepers take great risks and should be remembered for their sacrifices. Although it was against the rules to embellish things in our logbooks, I wrote in mine that there were nine bodies from the Buffalo 461 aboard that particular trip, on Hercules 307. That was my way of remembering them.

Master Warrant Officer William Munden (Ret) joined the air force in 1956 and served for thirty-two and a half years. During his career, he was stationed at Winnipeg, Comox, Trenton, and Victoria and flew on a wide variety of aircraft. In 1983, he became a civilian pilot and a glider pilot. He retired from the military in 1988. Bill lives with his wife, Nancy, in Mill Bay, B.C.

Me as a flight engineer sergeant in 1974.

Performing a water-rescue exercise with the Labrador helicopter in Comox.

Date	Hour	Aircraft Type and No.	Captain	Duty	Remarks (Including results of bombing, gunnery, exercises, etc.)	Flying Time Day	Flying Time Night
					442 T&R SQDN COMOX FEBRUARY 1971 (CONT)		
					CAPT DOUG STUART CAPT LYN WAGAR Time Carried Forward:— ▮▮ 5522.9		
9 FEB		CH-113 10402	CAPT WILLIS	F/E	PRINCE GEORGE XS - BOSTON BAR	3.1	
"		"	" "	"	BOSTON BAR - XX ABBOTSFORD	0.8	
"		"	" "	"	ABBOTSFORD VANCOUVER XX - VR - QQ COMOX	1.3	
12 FEB		CH-113 10402	CAPT WILLIS	F/E	COMOX QQ - ADF TRIALS - QQ COMOX	1.4	
18 FEB		CH-113 10404	CAPT CHARLAND	F/E	COMOX QQ - PILOT RECOVERY FROM VOODO - QQ COMOX Thanks. Doug Stuart Voodoo Pilot	0.7	STUART WAGAR SIGNED - 13½ years later.
18 FEB		CH-113 10404	CAPT CHARLAND	F/E	COMOX QQ - WRECKAGE LOCATION - QQ COMOX	0.5	
18 FEB		CH-113 10404	CAPT CHARLAND	F/E	COMOX SANDSPIT QQ - ZP-CANCELLED - QQ COMOX	1.9	
21 FEB		CH-113 10404	MAJ WESTON	F/E	COMOX PRINCETON QQ - MOUNTAIN RESCUE - DC	2.3	
22 FEB		CH113 10404	MAJ WESTON	F/E	PRINCETON DC - YF PENTICTON	0.7	
"		"	" "	"	PENTICTON YF - QQ COMOX	2.4	
23 FEB		CH-113 10402	MAJ WESTON	F/E	COMOX QQ - PATERSON LAKE - QQ COMOX	1.3	
25 FEB		CH-113 10402	CAPT WILLIS	F/E	COMOX QQ - SEARCH (CANCELLED) - QQ COMOX	0.5	
~~25 FEB~~		~~CH-113 10404~~	~~CAPT WILLIS~~	~~F/E~~	~~QQ - LOCAL - QQ~~	~~1.0~~	
					TOTAL TIME ▮▮ 5539.8		

The page of my logbook noting the Voodoo rescue. Doug's signature is on the line below.

The ceremony for the Buffalo Nine in Damascus, August 11, 1974.

YEAR 19.74.				AUGUST 1974		Time Brought Forward	7229.4	137.6
DATE		AIRCRAFT		CAPTAIN	DUTY	REMARKS AND RESULTS	FLYING TIME	
Month	Day	Type	No.				Day	Night
AUG	1	C-130	130328	UMBACH	F.E.	GOOSE BAY - LAHR	4.9	4.5
AUG	2	C-130	130315	UMBACH	F.E.	LAHR - AKROTIRI	4.6	2.5
AUG	2	C-130	130315	UMBACH	F.E	AKROTIRI - LAHR	5.8	
AUG	4	C-130	130315	UMBACH	F.E.	LAHR - AKROTIRI	3.0	3.0
AUG	4	C-130	130315	UMBACH	F.E.	AKROTIRI - LAHR	5.7	
AUG	5	C-130	130328	UMBACH	F.E.	LAHR - GOOSE BAY	10.7	
AUG	5	C-130	130328	UMBACH	F.E.	GOOSE BAY - TRENTON	4.0	
AUG	7	C-130	130306	MAJ DONALD	F.E.	TRENTON - LAHR	7.2	4.0
AUG	8	C-130	130307	CLARK	F.E.	LAHR - PRESTWICK	3.0	
AUG	8	C-130	130307	CLARK	F.E.	PRESTWICK - LAHR	3.0	
AUG	10	C-130	130307	CLARK	F.E.	LAHR - PISA	1.8	
AUG	10	C-130	130307	CLARK	F.E.	PISA - AKROTIRI	1.8	3.0
AUG	10	C-130	130307	CLARK	F.E.	AKROTIRI - CAIRO	2.3	
AUG	11	C-130	130307	CLARK	F.E	CIARO - DAMASCUS	1.0	2.0
AUG	11	C-130	130307	CLARK	F.E.	DAMASCUS - LAHR	7.3	BUFFALO CRASH VICTIMS AND THIS FLIGHT
AUG	14	C-130	130307	CLARK	F.E	LAHR - CAIRO	6.7	
AUG	14	C-130	130307	CLARK	F.E	CAIRO - LAHR	7.1	
AUG	16	C-130	130325	CLARK	F.E.	LAHR - KEFLAVIK	6.0	
AUG	16	C-130	130325	CLARK	F.E	KEFLAVIK - TRENTON	5.0	3.8
						TOTAL TIME	7320.3	160.4

(7367.0)
(7480.7)

The entries in my logbook for picking up the Canadians in the Buffalo Nine disaster.

The Hercules 307 in Ottawa in 2016.

151

From Wikwemikong to Cyprus

PRIVATE RON RIVERS (RET)

We were being deployed to Cyprus for a six-month UN peacekeeping tour. When I heard the news, I wasn't anxious like I thought I'd be. After being in the army for almost three years, I was excited to travel and see a new place, even though tensions were running high where we were headed.

I was born in 1957 on the Wikwemikong First Nations Reserve on Manitoulin Island. When I was growing up in the seventies, there weren't many options for jobs locally unless you worked in tourism. But I had an itch to do something else.

One day, I was watching TV and a commercial for the Canadian Armed Forces kept coming on. Because of the Cold War, there was a real push to recruit. I went out and picked up some pamphlets and learned that the military offered training in any trade. The 1976 Olympics in Montreal were still a few years away when someone mentioned to me that the military would probably do security. I'd never seen the Olympics, but I thought, *Hey, this might be a chance to see a bit of the world and get some skills.* So away I went and enlisted. My life would never be the same after that moment.

At the recruiting office, I took an aptitude test and told them I was interested in the infantry. As I signed the papers, I remember thinking, *What if I am deployed? What if we go to war?* I was nervous about that possibility, but eager to start something new. I felt strongly about serving my country and I knew I was making the right decision.

The recruiters arranged a bus ticket to Ottawa and a plane to Cornwallis, Nova Scotia, where I would begin my four months of basic training. I had never been that far away from home or for that long. I had never even been on a plane!

At four o'clock in the morning, we landed in Nova Scotia. An NCO (noncommissioned officer) rounded up those who had flown in, and we drove a couple of hours to the base, where we met up with the rest of the recruits, about 150 in total.

The first twenty-four hours were a whirlwind and a shock. I was young, inexperienced, and to be honest, still learning English. As they gave us our uniforms and showed us our accommodations, I had a hard time keeping up. I felt lost even though I was surrounded by so many people who were probably feeling a little bit of what I was.

After that first day, I thought, *What the hell did I do?* Then I reminded myself that I wanted this, that I had thought about this decision over and over. *Don't give up*, I said to myself. *You can do this.*

It was overwhelming, but I enjoyed it, especially the PT. We did a lot of running and calisthenics. I was young and in good shape and found it very fun. One of our tests was to finish a mile in under twelve minutes. I started with a time of eleven and a half, and after all the retests, I was down to eight minutes.

And once I settled in more to the routine, I became less shy. I was more open to walking up to someone new and talking to them, which is something I never did before. My training gave me a lot of confidence.

There was a big influx of recruits, so much so that the military was putting a new company into training each week. Our training was eleven weeks, with the last two falling over Christmas and New Year's, when everyone was scheduled to be home. Instead of spending the money to bring everyone back for just two weeks, they jammed our eleven-week course into eight weeks. To fill the gaps, we trained at night.

In training, anyone who falls behind gets re-coursed. Basically, that person has to start over from week one. Usually this happens in the first few weeks, but around my fifth week, the flu was making the rounds through our base, and I got sick. My throat was raw and I felt dizzy. I went to the MIR and they gave me some painkillers, but I was too fatigued to keep up. They told me that if I couldn't continue, I would be re-coursed. A lot of guys there were getting re-coursed, but none as far along as I was. I was more than halfway through training and I was being sent back to week one. I was heartbroken.

The following Monday, I was still not in top shape, but I went to meet my new group. My new sergeant, Sergeant McPhee, was a tough but fair leader, and he knew where I was starting over from.

He pulled me aside and said, "I hope you're not thinking about wanting to go home. Because you came this far, and you might as well see it through. This is the hardest part of the military, adjusting to it." He continued, "You're going to meet a lot of good friends in your career in the military."

Not a lot of our instructors took the time to give pep talks, but Sergeant McPhee did. And his encouragement meant the world of difference to me. He saw that I belonged there even when I felt like a failure. I took his advice, buckled down for training, and trusted that everything would be fine.

Going through training again, I knew what to expect and everything came easier. And we had eleven weeks. This time, I was able to help some other guys too. There was one recruit who had a hard time adjusting to some of the standards for cleanliness and order, so I showed him how to polish his boots, how to make his bed for inspection. He would miss little things, but I helped him spot those.

And he was by my side when we graduated eleven weeks later. I saw my training all the way through. Sergeant McPhee was right—this was just the beginning.

After that, a bunch of guys and I went to Wainwright, Alberta, for infantry training, which was a lot of the same stuff from basic, but harder. They did more outside training like patrols, and they showed us our personal weapons, how they worked. We cleaned them every day. Everyone kept saying, "We did this in Cornwallis." After a while, the instructor got pretty mad and shouted back, "This isn't Cornwallis!"

This time I really wanted to succeed. Right from the start, I was determined to put everything I had into it. There were so many tests right until the very last week, so there was always a slim chance that I just might not make it. It was only when I was marching in the graduation parade that it really sunk in that I'd reached my goal. We started off with forty-nine and graduated with fourteen.

After graduation I was posted to Calgary as part of 1 PPCLI. A lot of guys thought the training would ease off, that they'd be getting an easier go now that they were stationed at a battalion, but I told them, "You know, we're in the infantry, there is no such thing as easing out. We're going to keep training all the way through our careers."

And that's what happened when we got there. They started giving us more courses, different courses. There were no inspections, but we still had to keep everything clean and tidy, which was no problem for me. My basic training had given me that sense of discipline.

Right off the bat, they gave us a course in riot control and told us that we'd be using these skills for the Montreal Olympics. Ha, I couldn't believe it! I hadn't said anything about wanting to go, but there I was boarding a plane to Montreal.

We arrived a few weeks before the games started and trained for crowd control in the stadium, but we also toured around the city. I'm a big baseball fan, so we caught a couple of games at Jarry Park. And we checked out the nightlife too. During the games, we were pretty busy, always doing checks and security, but we would pop into events for a few minutes. I remember seeing some of the divers perform from amazing heights.

I had a couple of military friends that lived close to my family on Manitoulin Island. After the games, we got some time off, so I caught a ride with a couple of them and headed home for our leave of twenty days.

———

I returned to Wainwright in the fall and continued Cold War training for all of 1977. We did a lot of battle simulations, and went up to Suffield, Alberta, for three weeks of live-fire exercises with the British military. That's when we heard Elvis Presley had died. The world was changing.

When we returned to Wainwright, I saw Sergeant McPhee from a distance. He was probably a warrant officer by then. I wanted to go over and shake his hand and thank him for his advice back in basic, but I was in the middle of an exercise. By the time I looked back, he was gone.

A few weeks later, they told us we were being deployed to Cyprus for a six-month UN peacekeeping tour. When I heard the news, I wasn't anxious like I thought I'd be. After being in the army for almost three years, I was excited to travel and see a new place, even though tensions were running high where we were headed.

We landed in early April and immediately saw signs of the conflict between the Turks and the Greeks. All the buildings around us were shot up and old vehicles were partially blown away. There was peace, but it was shaky.

Our battalion was stationed at the Ledra Palace Hotel right on the Green Line between the two sides. There was a prison close to us, on the Greek side, but in the buffer zone. One day, we heard shots coming from that direction. My platoon NCO got his driver and took off to see what was happening. By then, we'd heard a bunch of shots. And on the Turkish side, we could see they had their guns pointed everywhere, ready to fire at any moment.

We needed to protect our area, so we loaded up our weapons and got into the trenches. Then we waited.

It was nighttime when my NCO returned and told us that one of the inmates at the prison had got a hold of a guard's gun and was trying to shoot his way out of jail. We were on an island, so I don't know where he thought he was going to go even if he did escape. With the odd gunfire coming from the prison itself, we knew the Turks thought the Greeks were coming across the Green Line for a battle. It was pitch-black, but we needed to diffuse the situation so that one side didn't attack the other under false presumptions.

My NCO got me and two other guys to go up to meet the Turks. Those trigger-happy Turks. With our flashlights in hand, we approached cautiously and just kept saying, "UN, UN." At first we couldn't find anyone who spoke English, but we finally did and told them what the situation was. They refused to stand down until the gunfire stopped. We had done all we could do, but we couldn't force them to stand down. Such is peacekeeping.

We kept moving to the other sentries, letting them know what was going on. There were also some British people that lived right in the buffer zone. When we knocked on their door, we discovered that they had just flown in from Germany. They didn't seem too concerned. One of them said, "How interesting."

Eventually, we heard they found the prisoner and everything calmed down a bit, but the tension between the two sides never really abated the whole tour.

When my tour finished, I came back and remained in the infantry until 1979. I stayed in Alberta for a few years working, then moved back to Manitoulin Island to be closer to my family. I got married and had kids.

In 2015, my youngest son went into the Black Bear Program, which is an Aboriginal military program where kids go through a six-week course—not as intense as basic—to see if they have a taste for the military. My wife and I attended my son's graduation at CFB Gagetown, New Brunswick, and I was so impressed with how much he had learned in six weeks. He's still in high school right now, but I'm trying to sway him to go into the military when he's done.

A couple of years ago, I found Sergeant McPhee on Facebook. I didn't think he would remember me, but I contacted him anyway and told him how his encouraging words helped me through basic training. He didn't remember who I was, but was glad I had gotten in touch. We keep in contact now.

Before I joined the military, I didn't really care much about my life or what I was doing, but all that changed. The military gave me a sense of purpose, straightened me out, and made me feel like I was a part of something.

Private Ron Rivers (Ret) grew up on the Wikwemikong First Nations Reserve on Manitoulin Island. He joined the Canadian Armed Forces in 1974 and served as a UN peacekeeper in Cyprus, for which he received two medals, UNICYP (United Nations Peacekeeping Force in Cyprus) and CPSM (Canadian Peacekeeping Service Medal). Ron was awarded the Aboriginal Veteran Millennium Medal, created by the National Aboriginal Veterans Association and the Department of Indigenous and Northern Affairs to commemorate those Aboriginals who volunteered to serve and defend Canada. He lives in Wikwemikong with his wife and two children.

During basic training, my group went to Granville Range to practice patrolling and range firing. I'm in the first row on the far left.

LEFT: My graduation photo at Cornwallis. I was very happy to pass.

BELOW: In Suffield, doing our live-fire training. I was in charge of the weapons detachment. Here I am with an anti-tank 84mm Carl Gustav and a 70mm mortar.

Just Another Day in Rwanda

Major Tim Isberg (Ret)

I had to have faith that the "blue beret" and a
military uniform would offer a form of passage and
protection.

In the summer of 1994, I arrived in Rwanda as a UN military observer (UNMO). I had been preparing to go to Mozambique, but a few weeks before my deployment, I was notified that my mission had changed. I was now going to Rwanda as part of the UN Assistance Mission in Rwanda—UNAMIR—for a one-year tour of duty. I was thirty-two, a captain, and this would be my first operational tour.

In 1994, the Canadian military was deployed on multiple UN operations, most simultaneously, and mission-specific training for UNMOs was in its early days. As an army officer in the artillery with some solid experience in the field and in airborne and airmobile operations in Canada and abroad, I had the general skills required to be a military observer. Along with several other Canadian UNMOs destined for various missions around the globe, I arrived in Kingston for a week of first-aid refreshers, and briefings on intelligence and medical advisories; geography and culture; familiarity with UN and non-governmental organizations, etc. UNMOs are unarmed, so refresher training on weapons and rules of engagement (ROE) were not part of the schedule. I attended all specific sessions for Mozambique, so when I was later told I would be deploying to Rwanda for UNAMIR, I didn't fully know what to expect.

There was a lot of turmoil internationally in the mid-nineties, and the media was very much focused on war in the former Yugoslavia. By the time I received my new orders in July and deployed that summer, I was generally aware of the atrocious mass killings and the battles between Rwandan Government Forces (RGF) and the Rwandan Patriotic Front (RPF). I also knew that a humanitarian situation had exploded in Rwanda since Rwandan President Habyarimana's plane was shot down on April 6, 1994. I didn't know, however, what the hell I was supposed to be doing, *specifically*, once I arrived.

In August, I and the nine other Canadian UNMOs who would later become some of my closest friends linked up in Nairobi. The next day, along with new incoming UNAMIR Force Commander Major General Guy Tousignant, a few NGOs, a *Time* magazine photographer, all of our luggage, a UN High Commissioner for Refugees (UNHCR) Land Cruiser, and other assorted odds and sods, we boarded a CAF Hercules for Rwanda. We made the steep, tactical approach and landed at the nearly destroyed Kigali airport. We were met by General Roméo Dallaire himself, a few fellow Canadian UNMOs, and a few key staff from General Dallaire's HQ who had just endured a hundred days of horrible chaos and were, I think, eager to meet some new faces. We reported to UNAMIR headquarters (formerly the Amahoro Hotel) based in Kigali near the infamous stadium.

There was a lot of confusion for us over those first several tiring and trying days. The day prior to our trip, we met at National Defence HQ in Ottawa to receive updated briefings that didn't actually clarify much at all; even our roles as UNMOs in theatre and our administration and benefits seemed to be less clear than ever. To add to the scenario, much of the new UNAMIR mission was undergoing significant change and expansion in a country still in the midst of devastation, with needs that far exceeded capabilities. The ten of us were simply a small cog in a wheel already going a hundred miles per hour.

Eventually, General Dallaire sorted out with his Canadian and UN counterparts that we were indeed needed as military observers and that we would be employed in various interim roles until more personnel arrived and our team locations were confirmed. After a week in Kigali, I was transferred to Butare prefecture in the south of Rwanda, where I was part of a small team assigned to set up a forward tactical HQ for Dallaire. The forward "Tac HQ" was to better assist in coordinating humanitarian needs and military liaising with the newly ensconced Rwandan Patriotic Army (RPA), a name change from their former RPF moniker. We were also to monitor French commando and French Foreign Legion withdrawal from Zone Turquoise, a military deployment that had been unilaterally actioned by the French government outside of a UN mandate. That action and its outcomes are another story in themselves.

Duties in the Tac HQ involved monitoring radio field reports, observing and reporting on military activity, reporting mass graves, and investigating new reported killings and massacre sites. I also regularly liaised with the RPA and coordinated and participated in meetings with a variety of UN agencies such as UNHCR and UNICEF, and also the International Committee of the Red Cross (ICRC) and various NGOs.

Before I joined the military, I happened to have had some formal law enforcement training and policing experience and had even been a part-time paramedic. So, combined with my army training, I had pretty good exposure to investigating and evidence gathering, reporting, liaising, and dealing with fatalities; but nothing could have prepared me for the *scale* of death and destruction in Rwanda. Here, the still fresh remnants of the genocide, its victims still strewn about, mass graves and burned-out villages; the continuous moving chain of millions of displaced people packed together slowly making their way through jungle and over volcanic mountain passes; the new killings, massacre sites, and mass graves; the prisons packed to standing room only, some with women and children; and finally, the daily scenes of poverty and fear, were brightened only by the underlying beauty of Rwanda's landscape and the smiles of children with outstretched hands you had to pass by without stopping. I didn't have to witness the genocidal act to understand the gravity of what took place. Nor could I escape the carnage. It was everywhere.

Rwanda, from the air, looks like an upside-down egg carton covered in banana trees and tea plantations, and it truly is, a "land of a thousand hills." Driving around the country is very dangerous because the vehicles driven by locals often have no or poor brakes and no windshields; the drivers have little experience; and the terrain is a perilous mix of hills, mountains, and jungle. I liked to define pavement in Rwanda as a road held together with potholes. And when it rains in Rwanda, it really rains. The powder-orange dirt turns to bright-red mud, and even paved roads become extremely slippery because they are coated with leaked oil and diesel. Combined with balding tires, it's a recipe for disaster as evidenced by the crashed vehicles rusting in several ravines throughout the country. And when it's nighttime in the forest villages, it's not just dark, it's a thick blanket of black that drapes itself over everything. Other than edgy moments with the nervous trigger fingers of young RPA soldiers, and the occasional cross-fire incidents, the risks became routine. However, a related danger was becoming complacent to that norm. Incidents involving mines and crude IEDs weren't on my or anyone else's radar until one day in Cyangugu.

––––––––

By mid-November 1994, I transferred to Cyangugu, a prefecture deep in southwestern Rwanda, known for almost constant criminal and insurgent activity and suspected reprisal killings by RPA.

Cyangugu town and Kamembe airfield were the main centres of interest, and even though there was no major battle there, many buildings were destroyed and had no roofs, windows, doors, or fixtures. These were all stolen and had disappeared with those who had escaped across the border. Cyangugu borders the (now) Democratic Republic of the Congo, which at that time was Zaire, and shares a large portion of its border down the middle of Lake Kivu. At the south end of Lake Kivu, Bukavu's border-crossing with Cyangugu town is across the Ruzizi River, literally rifle-shot distance from hundreds of thousands of refugees and a good chunk of escaped RGF and Interahamwe (a militia group) responsible for the genocidal rampage months earlier. Needless to say, I ended up very close to where the enemy had escaped. Machine gun firefights between the insurgents and the RPA, or with Zaire's military, were not uncommon.

During and immediately after the genocide, the RPA proved that they were a very capable force by quickly conquering the RGF and pushing them and the Interahamwe westward toward Zaire. They were eager to complete this push, but by early fall '94, much of southwest Rwanda was still being temporarily occupied and protected from the RPA by the French army forces in Zone Turquoise. When the French withdrew, the RPA quickly filled the entire sector with forces and seized control and authority. They proved relatively capable of handling some insurgent activity, but also took aggressive action and arrested locals—mainly Hutus—and the jails quickly filled beyond capacity. UNAMIR needed UNMOs and UN troops to monitor, report, and assist in a myriad of activities and incidents in an area where things had a tendency to get worse before they got better.

I was positioned with Sector 4-Charlie, and the house in Cyangugu that I lived in doubled as the sector headquarters and housed a few other UNMOs, hailing from Mali, India, Nigeria, and eventually others. Unlike most Canadian soldiers who deploy, UNMOs are not housed or secured within a contingent camp. We found our own food, lodging, and security. Initially, our house had no working plumbing, no electricity, and no glass in many of the windows. We put up some screens to keep the mosquitoes out because cerebral malaria was a concern (and we knew one Ghanaian UNMO who had died).

The UN was slow to get us supplies, but we were resourceful and figured out how to get what we needed. Food was a challenge, not just because it was hard to obtain in those early months but also because in our household there was a mix of ethnic and religious customs where Hindu, Muslim, and Christian could not necessarily eat the same meal, but we made it work.

Vehicles, the main enabler for us to investigate and observe and attend meetings, were extremely inadequate and left many teams unable to effectively patrol. Our team had two 4Runner-type vehicles, which we inherited from Cambodia and Somalia UN missions, so these were in rough shape, especially the tires. And there were rarely spares.

My work in Cyangugu was similar to that in Butare, but I was assigned the prominent role of humanitarian affairs cell officer and was responsible for coordinating UNAMIR efforts with those of multiple NGOs and other UN and international agencies, and liaising with ICRC occasionally. Médecins du Monde (MDM), Hôpital Sans Frontière (HSF), and Médecins Sans Frontière (MSF) were three such NGOs, running a mix of clinics, hospitals, and orphanages. I worked very closely with MDM, the main NGO in this region. They did a lot of good work, but were sometimes targeted for attack. In January 1995, a main orphanage in Kamembe was ambushed by armed men, and many of the staff and children were injured and killed. I had visited that orphanage a couple of weeks prior for a children's party, and one of the children I took a picture of was one of the victims. I have a journal entry from the day of the ambush that reads, "This never really bothered me until I started writing about it."

I travelled extensively throughout the back roads of Cyangugu and established some good relations with local RPA and interim government officials at various levels. As a native English speaker who could speak French and had some basic Swahili abilities, I ended up regularly assisting UN tribunal and special investigators, and also UN human rights teams who were helping establish a justice system. I was still assisting in genocide research on mass graves and timeline facts, but due to the quantity of new incidents, I was regularly called to investigate recent killings and massacre sites. These killings always fell into one of three categories: local banditry, insurgent attacks, or RPA.

RPA had, by then, been suspected of using intimidation and violence on many local villages. If someone in the RPA was deemed responsible for a murder or massacre, the leadership might or might not admit it, and might or might not take corrective action. Things were getting more political too. Intimidation by RPA and restrictions on movement of UN and NGO communities became the norm. Later, there were a growing number of incidents of theft and violence against UN and NGO personnel. UNAMIR was supposed to have unlimited movement, but we would often encounter RPA roadblocks where soldiers armed with AK-47s would either cock their weapons right in front of us or shoot live rounds in our direction as a scare tactic. Sometimes restriction to a certain site or area was just a control measure by soldiers, who were hiding military movements and weapon systems or criminal acts.

I had to have faith that the "blue beret" and a military uniform would offer a form of passage and protection. Despite growing RPA disdain for UNAMIR, RPA senior soldiers and officers could still respect a fellow military officer, blue beret or not. I was unarmed, so having good interpersonal skills was another important asset for effecting change while protecting myself. At times I would have to bite my tongue and find a superior officer to try to communicate with when things got testy. I often thought, *If I get mad, I'll definitely risk being shot.*

On March 31, 1995, Captain Gord Hagar from the Canadian contingent came to our sector by helicopter for a familiarization visit and briefing. The small Canadian contingent was by that time responsible for much of the logistics to all of UNAMIR. As a Canadian, I was obliged to support the visit and get him back to Kamembe airfield for a prearranged pickup. Along with my fellow UNMO from Uruguay, a captain who went by the nickname Zapato, I planned on taking Captain Hagar on a short drive in Cyangugu town, to our Sector HQ house for a briefing, then back to the helipad so he could return to Kigali. Zapato and I would then continue on to visit an orphanage in Rusayo and an MDM clinic in Mblizi.

Unfortunately, the rain was heavy off and on that day, and the low haze from the charcoal makers was so dense that Hagar's return flight was delayed and eventually cancelled. Since he couldn't go anywhere, I suggested that he come with us on our patrol and see what a UNMO does on a typical day. I could see the trepidation in his countenance, but he gamely agreed and we planned to set off after lunch if the muddy roads and conditions were favourable.

We parked at a typical café along the roadside. I use the word "café" loosely—it was essentially a roadside niche with stolen UNHCR tarps cut into umbrella shapes; tables and chairs; and a crude charcoal cooker somewhere out of sight. The weather didn't look like it was going to improve, and we'd likely be sitting this day out so I ordered goat on a stick, some fried bananas, and a beer. Captain Hagar's eyes got a little bigger when he saw that I was going to eat local food *and* consume a beer, but I explained to him that this was normal for us, that we were essentially going off duty, and unlike his fellow Canadians in Kigali, we never had a contingent's kitchen or cooks to stock and prepare our food. We UNMOs ate local or not at all.

After an hour, the weather had barely improved, and it was getting too late to patrol out to Rusayo or Mblizi and still make it back before dark. Before we could return to our house, I received a sudden, frantic call on the radio from Céline, one of the MDM staff. She was short of breath and near tears. She had heard from another MDM staff member that there was an explosion on the road to the Mblizi clinic. She knew I was supposed to visit the clinic that day and pleaded with me to find out what had happened. It was common for passengers, and patients, to cram into the open backs of small pickup trucks for transport, and Céline was worried that someone had thrown or fired a grenade at a passing MDM truck coming back from the clinic.

I radioed the Ethiopian battalion that had a few of its elements in that area, and with some trepidation, headed to the clinic with Zapato and Captain Hagar. After a half-hour drive, we were off the paved road and onto the clinic back road in the forest, and the route was far more dangerous given our balding tires, the muddy, hilly terrain, and the impending darkness. We didn't know exactly what the incident was, or where it occurred, only that it was somewhere this side of the Mblizi clinic.

We made our way as best we could and the shadows began to grow longer. We were going around a sharp corner, still a few kilometres from the clinic, when my headlights flashed onto a UN vehicle from the Ethiopian battalion. One of the soldiers waved frantically to stop, so I brought the vehicle to the side of the road and we got out.

The air was damp, and I could taste the diesel fumes and acrid smoke that hung low to the ground. I couldn't understand the Ethiopian soldier, but as I walked towards him, he moved his hands in a cutting motion across his legs and pointed down the road. Beyond him I saw a few mud huts and the wreckage of a white MDM pickup truck several metres off the road. Wisps of steam were rising from engine parts and debris. As I came closer, I saw a large blackened hole in the middle of the road. The truck was lying on its side, and nearby were casualties and several locals who seemed to be tending wounds or simply observing.

In moments like these, you often react instantly, and then feel the fear later after your trained, reflexive muscle memory has dissipated and the adrenaline has left your body. I'd experienced a few of those moments by then. This was different. I'd been in Rwanda for almost eight months and had never seen an incident like this. It took several seconds for the scene in front of me to sink in, for me to realize that an explosive device, probably a land mine, had detonated under the truck. I looked down at my feet and thought, *We could all very well be in a minefield. Yeah, don't panic.*

In the corner of my eye, I noticed one of the Ethiopian soldiers stabbing his bayonet into the ground checking for mines, and that freaked me out because that's not the proper way to do the drill. The rest of his patrol remained at their vehicle, and it looked like they were about to leave, but I told them they were staying until we were all ready to go together.

There was a sort of quiet chaos all around, some crying and whimpering. The sun had almost completely disappeared and it was becoming more difficult to see, but I advanced carefully towards one of the bodies. It was a woman wrapped in banana leaves by the locals. She was deceased, but the baby with her was miraculously still alive!

I looked around and saw others in shock, sitting with broken limbs and cuts. Help wasn't coming for anyone, including us. Locals were walking on the scene and a few cows were wandering nearby; the site was already full of muddy footprints and no secondary explosions had gone off. Cautiously, but quickly, Captain Hagar, Zapato, and I began to triage. In that moment, our sole aim was to get the hell out of there and onward to the Gihundwe Hospital in Cyangugu as soon as we could.

We couldn't take everyone, but we did load two women (one with life-threatening injuries to her leg), the baby, and a man into the back of the 4Runner vehicle, and then I jumped in the driver's seat. It was a very enclosed space, and the cries and the smell of blood, vomit, and shit invaded the whole vehicle, even our clothing. I knew the area we were in could contain more mines, so with Zapato feeling the ground behind each tire, I carefully manoeuvred the truck to turn it around. The whole thing seemed so . . . ridiculous, stupid, surreal, and somehow, urgently necessary.

It was near complete darkness, and the Ethiobat vehicle was in front of me for the drive out. I tried to stay in its tracks—at a distance—thinking that would be safest in case there were more mines on the same road that we just drove over to get there. That thought made me wonder, "Did we actually miss any mines on the drive into the site?" I was scared for all of us, but at least I could concentrate on driving.

By then it was pitch-black. Because of the short, steep hills and our gutless vehicle with such a heavy load, I had to speed down each slippery slope to make it up the next one, and every time I did, I risked colliding with the Ethiobat vehicle in front of me. Luckily, we made it to the hospital without incident. No drama (insert nervous laugh here)! We had radioed ahead, and on arrival we carried the woman with the wounded leg and the baby right into treatment. Her injury was so bad that after only half an hour, she had already had her leg amputated.

The next day, we heard of four more people injured by an antipersonnel mine that exploded only four metres from where we had been standing at the wreckage. We also pieced together that on that fateful day, a local driver hired by the MDM was transporting nine people that required medical treatment from the MDM clinic to the Gihundwe Hospital in Cyangugu. Based on the remnants of a cow scattered across the road, we figured that the cow had tripped what was likely an antipersonnel mine around three o'clock in the afternoon. A couple hundred metres away, the MDM truck hit a single anti-tank mine buried in the road. More explosives were later discovered planted nearby. By whom, we didn't know, but they were likely set up to disrupt NGO and RPA activity, perhaps to cause continued instability and keep the government and local RPA on edge.

There was no evidence to suggest that there had been a specific target, including us, and I was unable to ever confirm if the mine was a blind hit, or if it was triggered or observed by the bad guys with eyes on the site. I learned in investigating killings that it was sometimes the case that the killers were actually there with you, standing in the crowd, watching and listening to what people would say, using their presence to keep witnesses quiet. I couldn't help but wonder if someone had been watching us mill about in the carnage.

The MDM vehicle and ours were the only vehicles known to be on that road that day, at that time. Given the time of the explosion, in our intended patrol, our vehicle would have driven over that same spot en route to visit the clinic before the MDM truck even set out. Had we not stopped and waited out the weather at that makeshift roadside café, it could have been us that hit the mine.

I thank my lucky stars we survived that day, and now I joke that a beer saved my life.

––––––––

In some ways my first UN mission felt like trial by fire. I mean, Rwanda wasn't your typical UN mission by a long shot. At the time, Sector 4-Charlie in Cyangugu was known for being a place that no one was jumping up and down to be deployed. But it was what it was, and we got used to it. Even with the working conditions and ever-present dangers, I made fast friends with my fellow UNMOs and the NGOs, and for years after, we kept in touch. As for Sector 4-C, it was like family to me. You bond quickly in these circumstances.

My mission in Rwanda was much more than the typical blue-beret-and-binocular routine that many Canadians think of when they hear the word "peacekeeping." A year is long. I learned a lot. I came back a bit different, but better for it. Even amid all that violence and hate, we witnessed signs of recovery; and when I saw those smiling children with outstretched hands waving, I felt that somehow we were making a difference. And that's what helps me sleep at night.

Major Tim Isberg (Ret) joined the Canadian Armed Forces in 1985. He served as a peacekeeper in Rwanda, where he was awarded a Canadian Chief of Defence Staff Commendation for his actions on March 31, 1995. He has since been on multiple military deployments and duties in Europe and throughout the Middle East and the Levant, and Afghanistan. He has run a NATO literacy program, overseen UN military field operations, and worked in investigative and mediation roles and in senior political-military liaison capacities. Tim is also an accomplished singer-songwriter, and his album *Tears Along the Road* was selected by Music Canada as a Top 25 Favourite Album of 2015. Tim currently resides in Sherwood Park, Alberta.

Enjoying a lighter moment in Rwanda, 1994.

> 15 Aug, flew into Kigali flt 810 (Cdn Herc) with some NGO
> pers, Time Photographer Louise Gubb (S. Africa)
> UNHCR Land Cruiser + all our luggage, etc. New
> Force Comd & DCos (Col Anp) also on board. On
> landing, small ceremony + lts of media since
> When Dallaire + DCmd met new force Comd.
>
> Kigali + Butare both have neither running
> water, power or sewage system. Our accn at
> Canada One is residences of Belgian Village - very
> nice before the war. Meals are currently still
> hard rats (German). Market downtown is starting
> to open up for local purchase / eat ... if you dare
> We attended Polish Happy Hr before rtn to
> Belgian Village night of the 15th. None of us slept
> well, since our bodies are still so screwed

Here is a journal passage from the day we arrived in Kigali, August 15, 1994.

Activities in 4C are becoming increasingly unstable. Dozen(+) attacks by militia/RHF in last 2 weeks plus other acts of Banditti RPA stupidity, etc. The most disturbing incident was the attack on one of the orphanages administered by MDM. Here, on 3-4 Jan, grenades+ rifles were used against those helpless kids. 21 injured, 4 serious, 1 dead. I was just there last week @ x-mas watching them sing and dance + even took some pictures. Didn't seem to bother me so much until I was scribing all the details for a report to Kigali.

I realize now how sudden+ dangerous mines can be, and me+ my friends are very lucky. On 31 March myself + Zapato were to go to Rusayo and MBILIZI. It rained so hard and because we only had our veh for a few hours, I elected to postphone our patrol. We would have been on the road to MBILIZI between 1530-1630 after visiting Rusayo orphanage earlier in the afternoon after lunch. We in fact had planned to be out the whole day, but Capt Gord Hagar's Heli was delayed, delayed again, and finally cancelled altogether. Because of the know amount of mud at Rusayo, the difficulty patrolling North after MIBILIZI and that I still had Gord with me, we cancelled.

Two entries I made in my journal after I relocated to Cyangugu, from January 5 and April 6, 1995.

Patrolling in Bosnia

MASTER CORPORAL TREVOR SMITH (RET)

I knew I had been trained by some of the best, if not
the best, and I never feared what was going to happen
because I put a lot of faith in that training. I was
prepared to face any situation head-on.

I guess you could say the military is in my blood.

My grandfather served in an artillery unit in WWII, my dad served for three years before joining the Ontario Provincial Police, and my uncle Jim signed up in the early 1980s. He's now a colonel working at the embassy in Washington, but back when I was a kid, he was posted with 3 RCR (Royal Canadian Regiment) in Winnipeg. We lived in Ignace, Ontario, west of Thunder Bay, so he would visit us often and bring military swag like T-shirts. Needless to say, I was heavily influenced by my family. In 1995, after a year of college, I decided to follow in my family's footsteps and sign up myself.

Growing up with a police officer for a dad, I always had a disciplined lifestyle, so basic training wasn't a shock for me after twenty years of living under my dad's roof. I was used to getting up at 5:30 a.m., used to routine. The army was just an extension of how I was raised. And I really enjoyed it. The military instilled such a sense of pride in me and my work.

I finished basic training in Saint-Jean, Quebec, then went to battle school in Meaford, Ontario, to train to join the RCR. Right before my graduation ceremony at Meaford in 1997, I was waiting in the hallway outside the gym with my fellow grads and happened to see someone who looked like my uncle in the lobby. But the person quickly ducked into another room. I thought, *That looks like Uncle Jim, but no, he said he wasn't able to make it.*

Soon enough we began marching into the gym for parade, and wouldn't you know but my uncle Jim was standing there in the crowd in his dress uniform. I was overcome. After the ceremony, he came over and said, "I wasn't sure I could make it, but I didn't want to tell you I could, then disappoint you. When I found out I could come, I wanted to surprise you."

"So that was you I saw earlier?" I asked.

"Yeah, I wasn't paying attention," he laughed. "But when I turned, I saw you staring right at me."

We hugged and shook hands, and I knew he was proud of me. And I know if my grandpa had been alive, he'd have been pleased as well.

———

After graduation, I was posted to the 3 RCR in Petawawa. And a year later, I was notified of my first deployment to Bosnia. Unfortunately, I broke my hand just before the pre-deployment training, and was left off the list to go. But I was put in the 10 percent pool to replace anyone.

Just before Christmas 1998, I was on a driver course at my unit and a warrant officer came in and pulled me out of class. He shook my hand and said, "Congratulations, you've got four days, then you're leaving." My fiancée and I were getting ready for our first holiday together, but I had to replace a fella, so I went home and broke the news that I was leaving for a two-month stint.

Our role in Bosnia was stabilization; I knew we weren't going into combat, but I was nervous about what to expect. Was this going to be a real quiet time? Or something that goes off the rails quickly? Until you get your boots on the ground, you don't really know. But I knew I had been trained by some of the best, if not *the* best, and I never feared what was going to happen because I put a lot of faith in that training. I was prepared to face any situation head-on.

When I arrived, it was wintertime, and while Bosnia was a tad milder than Canada, the two countries actually looked a lot alike. There was snow on the ground and miles and miles of evergreen trees all throughout the countryside.

The biggest difficulty on my first tour was joining a team more than halfway through their tour. Of course, I knew a handful of them from training, but not all, and I wasn't para-qualified at the time like they were, so catching up and integrating myself into the group was the biggest hurdle. Other than that, my two months went by very quickly.

———

In early 2001, I redeployed as part of NATO SFOR (Stabilization Force) Operation Palladium, and again, our job was to ensure that certain areas in Bosnia were stable. This time, I was more at ease. I knew what to expect because I had trained with the whole battle group. All we had to focus on was ensuring a simple transition from the previous team, which involved introducing ourselves to the locals and letting them know that nothing would change from the previous six months.

The first day we arrived, we went to the Junior Ranks' mess bar to get our beer cards for our strict limit of two beers a day, and Mladin, the same bartender from my first tour, was there. I called out his name, and he remembered me! A lot of the locals who worked in the camp—our interpreters, our barber—were the same as from two years ago. So it was just a matter of getting settled in my bunk and our routine, and having at 'er!

I was stationed at Camp Maple Leaf in Zgon, about four kilometres from Ključ, with 4 Platoon, November Company, but there were many camps and outposts because our area of responsibility (AOR) was fairly large. Every day we would branch out for patrols, sometimes into the hills, sometimes into town. And every Saturday we patrolled the market in Ključ and made sure that there was no black-market activity. There was also a bar we used to patrol. I forget the name, but we called it the Purple Onion because it had purple signs. It was kind of surreal—we'd walk through the nightclub in our combats, our pistols on our hips, just to show the people that we didn't want any black-market stuff going on. The Bosnian military weren't allowed to train without observation, so we also inspected the cantonment site where they kept their weapons and ammunition. We'd do counts, make sure there wasn't anything missing and that the sites were secure.

One of the highlights of our tour was the humanitarian work we did. I remember this one family that lived in the hills about an hour's drive from our camp.

I'm a big dog lover and this family had a couple of dogs. The first time I visited them, they had this tiny little puppy, a Shepherd mix. It didn't have a name yet, so I asked them if I could name it, and they said yes. I named him after Nikita, my dog back home, and as the tour progressed I watched him grow from this teeny thing that I could hold in my arms to a sixty-pound dog. My wife even used to send me dog treats and toys to take to them.

We visited them frequently as they were rebuilding their family compound, and we tried to help them however we could. There were three houses on-site, but they were able to live in only two rooms in one of the houses because so much needed to be repaired.

They had a wood stove, but they didn't have enough chimney pipes to reach the ceiling, so they had set up their stove so that it was about four feet off the ground. I tried to get them an extra length or two of pipe, but didn't have any luck. Eventually I went to a sergeant, and he said that he would get us a brand new woodstove with about eighteen feet of pipe.

It was a pretty special day when our section arrived at their house with their new stove. I remember sitting with the grandmother of the family. She was patting my arm and speaking to me, and I could see our interpreter's eyes welling up, so I asked her what the woman was saying. She was thanking me for helping them and calling me her angel. I was floored. I was just so honoured to be able to help them.

As summer arrived, Bosnia became tremendously hot. Every day at noon, the PMed techs (Preventative Medicine technicians) would take weather readings, and there were days that it was thirty-five degrees, and close to fifty with the humidex. We had about forty guys in our platoon, and we were getting issued eleven hundred litre-and-a-half bottles of water a week. We slept four guys to one Weatherhaven tent inside an old carpet factory without air conditioning, so we would freeze our water bottles solid, and come bedtime we would stand them in our wash basins with a fan behind them just to get cool breeze. We'd try to take cold showers, but by the time we walked back from the showers, we were already soaked in sweat again.

It sounds pretty brutal, but honestly, I loved it. We got hot meals every day, and we had a ball hockey rink and a movie room. We'd have our two beers per day and maybe a Coke in the drinking mess. And we could buy snacks and stuff from the Canadian Forces Exchange System store (CANEX). We had everything we needed, and then some. Despite the heat, I knew we were living the high life compared to the people we were helping.

———

In late May, I set out on patrol with Private Steve Murgatroyd, Corporal Corey Stapleton, Corporal Martinson, and our interpreter, a young woman in her early twenties named Dragana. We were driving our six-wheel Grizzly APC (armoured personnel carrier) into Ključ, a predominately Muslim area, and when we reached the main intersection, we saw a demonstration of about fifty people. They were yelling and screaming and wouldn't let us through, but we had to pass through this intersection to go anywhere else in our AOR.

Dragana was very good at her job, very personable, so she gladly got out of the Grizzly and explained that we were going on patrol, but the protestors refused to let us through. She found out that there was a cornerstone-laying ceremony for a new mosque in Banja Luka, a nearby town that was predominately Christian, and several buses of people from Ključ had travelled to Banja Luka for the event. In protest to the mosque, Christian demonstrators were preventing the Ključ buses from returning home. Here at our Ključ intersection, the Muslim community was expressing their displeasure by forming a barricade of their own. And the crowd was getting bigger.

We got on the radio and informed our camp of the situation, but anyone would have to go right through this intersection to get to us. The only way around the intersection was to drive about forty-five minutes out of the way.

Corporal Martinson, or Marty, our acting patrol commander, said to us, "Let's just keep an eye on things."

There was nothing else we could do but wait. We didn't want any damage to happen, but we didn't want the protest to get out of control. Corey was our gunner, so he was poking out of the turret watching the crowd. Steve was our driver, so he had to stay in the front of the Grizzly. Marty and I remained on the ground.

The International Police Task Force (IPTF) had an office close to where we were in Ključ, and two officers who had been out on patrol came in behind us. When they saw the crowd, they jumped out of their vehicle.

"The protestors want something done," Dragana told them.

About half an hour had passed by then, and the crowd had swelled from 50 to 350 people. There was no way we could disperse them with our small group. Off to the left was a little park area with a Bosnian police station, so the IPTF officers took Dragana to the station to find out what we could do to quell the demonstration.

As the crowd expanded, we all put on our frag and tactical vests and I had my rifle in my patrol sling, which is a great piece of kit because it attaches the rifle to your body so no one can ever take your weapon from you. In the patrol sling, my rifle sat parallel to the ground, but at the front was a snap. If I needed to use my gun, all I had to do was undo the snap, and the sling would synch up around my shoulder, allowing me to ready my rifle.

While the IPTF officers and Dragana were gone, the protest escalated and the crowd flipped a car in the middle of the intersection. They were getting louder and more boisterous.

Marty said, "Listen, we need to get our interpreter back because we need to figure out what's going on."

He decided to walk around the crowd by way of the park. He had made it about three-quarters of the way past the edge of the demonstration when I saw him immediately turn around and come back rather quickly. He had a really strange look on his face.

"What's going on?" I asked.

"There's a weapon in the crowd. I just heard somebody cock a rifle."

In training, we're taught how to take apart weapons that we don't use and how to identify them, so we know all the sounds, especially the sound of a weapon being cocked.

Marty grabbed his rifle and got up in the commander's hatch to call back to camp and update them on our situation.

I looked up at Corey and said, "Close the hatch and power up the turret. Just swing it side to side to keep an eye on the crowd." We all knew the most important thing was to stay calm.

Just then we saw Dragana coming back with the IPTF officers. When they were maybe fifty to sixty feet from our Grizzly, at the edge of the crowd, I saw some people yell at her. It was a woman and three men. Dragana responded calmly in Serbo-Croat, and all of a sudden they got even angrier. Dragana was usually very happy-go-lucky, but in that moment, her demeanour changed completely.

The IPTF officers told us that the Bosnian police were working to come up with a plan to disperse the crowd, but the whole time we were talking, this irate woman kept yelling at Dragana.

I asked, "What's wrong?"

"This woman wants to take me," she replied.

"Take you? What do you mean?"

"They know I'm from Banja Luka. They can tell by my accent. They're saying they want to take me hostage." She started to cry.

"This is what you're going to do," I said. "You're going to crawl into the back of the Grizzly and lock the door." It was a beautiful day and we had all the hatches open in the back so we could stand up while we were driving. "Close the hatches and stay in there until we tell you to come out."

She rounded the back of the Grizzly, and I told Marty that things were getting worse.

He called back to camp again and asked for the Quick Reaction Force (QRF), a group of guys always ready to go at a moment's notice.

When he was on the radio, the woman and the three men, her nephews we discovered, approached the front of our Grizzly, and I could see the nephews were big lads and that they had pickaxe handles or clubs in their hands. I told them to stop, and they shouted something to us in Serbo-Croat.

Before Dragana closed the hatches, she said, "They're not going to stop until they get what they want."

I found out later that they had said, "We have to do what we have to do. We want that girl."

I knew a little bit of Serbo-Croat, not enough to have an actual conversation, but I told them as best I could to get back from the vehicle.

Steve was in the driver's seat, Corey in the turret, and Marty was still on the radio in the commander's hatch; the IPTF guys were unarmed, so it was just me. The crowd was only getting louder and we didn't know where that weapon was. I looked down at my patrol sling and undid the snap, then grabbed the forestock of my rifle and the pistol grip to show them that I wasn't kidding, that they had to back up.

But they continued to advance. I raised my rifle slightly, and the woman turned to her nephews and said something to them. They kept on coming until they were almost right in front of me. I raised my rifle to my shoulder and stuck the barrel into the woman's chest to push her backwards.

There were rules of engagement that we had to follow, so I hadn't cocked my rifle, but that would have been the next step if they came closer. And if they rushed me or tried to get past me to the Grizzly, I would have had to shoot, and I did not want to. My dad in all his years policing always said that when it comes to making a decision, he would rather be judged by twelve than carried by six.

Immediately, the woman's eyes widened and her nephews backed up. I pushed her about two paces backwards and said, "Stop, or I'll shoot." My heart was pounding and inside I was thinking, *Just please, please, back up. I don't want to pull the trigger.*

She went to turn to her nephews, but they were gone; they had just taken off. She looked back at me, said something I didn't understand, then retreated herself.

I lowered my rifle, and my heart began to slow.

After fifteen to twenty minutes, we backed up our vehicle slightly, made sure Dragana was okay, then let her out of the hatch. We were sitting two abreast, monitoring, monitoring, monitoring, when the QRF showed up shortly after. They had mobilized a bunch of troops on the base to be on the ready should things get even more out of hand, and they parked in the opposite lane so together we blocked the intersection.

The Bosnian police were also starting to arrest a few people for throwing stuff and being disruptive. As the day dragged on, the weather got crappy and we heard that the buses being held in Banja Luka were finally released. Gradually, the crowd started to trickle away, but we never did find that weapon. It wasn't until about ten or ten-thirty that we were allowed to pull out and leave. Our patrol started at three o'clock in the afternoon and we didn't leave until seven and a half hours later.

We took our time getting back to camp, then once there, we had to dress down the Grizzly, clean it and our weapons. With all the adrenaline surging through me, I didn't go to bed until two in the morning.

I reported the incident, but because I didn't cock my weapon or fire a round, there was nothing else I had to do. The only time we were allowed to do a quick escalation of force was to protect ourselves or mission-essential kit. As harsh as it may sound, interpreters were just that. We couldn't have done anything without them. They were our eyes and ears, a lifeline to knowing what was going on. And we treated them like they were one of our own. I had done what I needed to do to protect our interpreter, our equipment, and the guys with me.

A couple of weeks later, we heard that they were going to be redoing the cornerstone-laying ceremony, and the NATO commanders of Multi-National Division South-West wanted their forces to be ready to assist if need be. The Bosnian police were going to be doing crowd control, but if the protest escalated, we would be on hand. We did riot training at our camp, then during the night we drove to a staging area at an old soccer stadium.

At around seven in the morning, I was lying in the back of the Grizzly sleeping when we heard a *bang bang bang* on the door. It was our section 2IC.

"You guys have got to see this," he said. "No, no, stand on top of the Grizzly."

As far as you could see, there was nothing but armour and soldiers. NATO had deployed close to 2,500 troops from the Czech, British, and Canadian militaries, and there was enough armour to encircle a five-block radius.

Ironically, we ended up never being called in. It rained that day and the crowd that showed up to protest was quite a bit smaller than the number of Bosnian police officers monitoring them. Nevertheless, the response from the NATO commanders was incredible. They wanted to ensure what happened the last time didn't occur again.

An incident like that was quite rare. Our whole tour, the people that we interacted with were fantastic. We would sit with them and drink coffee, and we would help them rebuild in whatever way we could. I always say that 99 percent of the people there loved us, 0.99 percent were indifferent, and 0.01 percent hated us. The times we spent with the 99 percent outshine all the rest.

Unfortunately, we were in Bosnia when 9/11 happened. I did an early-morning patrol that day, showered, and went back to my bunk for a nap. Corey was right across the hall from me, and in the afternoon he woke me up and told me to come with him to the mess hall. We saw the news on the TV there, and we knew everything was going to change. Because there was and is such a stigma towards the Muslim community, our alert status went up. By the end of the day, we put our soft-skin Iltis vehicles away and got out the heavier equipment. We went from patrolling in regular combats to dressing in full combat gear with rifles and helmets. I was an M-203 gunner, so I also had to wear my 40mm grenade launcher and carry grenades. I felt bad for the Bosnian people who had grown accustomed to seeing us sitting across from them having a coffee at their own tables with just our pistols. Now we had to keep our distance. It was sad to see their reactions, but they understood why.

Other than that, I loved every minute of my tour. The people in Bosnia were wonderful and it was a beautiful place to be. After I returned home, I stayed with 3 RCR until 2002, then I re-mustered out of the infantry into what was called Fire Control Systems but is now known as the Electrical-Optronic Technicans. I trained in Kingston and Borden, then was posted back to Petawawa, where I served in four different units as a technician. I was promoted to master corporal in 2012 and finished my career as an electrical-optronic technician with the Royal Canadian Dragoons Armoured Unit.

In 2015, I was medically released due to severe arthritis in my hip and knees. It was time for this old guy to rest his bones and pack it in, to spend more time with my family. But I'll always cherish the time I spent with my brothers in the RCR. The camaraderie I had with them is what I miss most about the military life.

Master Corporal Trevor Smith (Ret) joined the military in 1995 and served for just under twenty years. During his career, he received the Canadian Peacekeeping Service Medal (CPSM), NATO Medal for Former Yugoslavia (NATO-FY), and a Canadian Forces Decoration. In his downtime, he rides his motorcycle. Trevor lives in Haley Station, Ontario, with his wife, Shelley, and their son, Aidan, and daughter, Danica.

Here I am in basic training in Saint-Jean in the fall of 1997. I have a poppy on my beret and a C-7 in my arms. I thought I was pretty cool at the time.

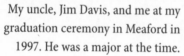

My uncle, Jim Davis, and me at my graduation ceremony in Meaford in 1997. He was a major at the time.

Celebrating the one-hundredth anniversary of the army base at Petawawa with a special visit from Governor General Adrienne Clarkson. I'm in front on the left.

Fighting Ebola in Sierra Leone

MASTER CORPORAL LISA OUELLETTE

Because we were completely covered, our voices were muffled and the only thing our patients saw were our eyes, so we wrote our names on the plastic sheet on our chests. I wrote "Medic Lisa."

Hydration. That's the most important thing I learned during the Ebola crisis. In our Sierra Leone clinic, we saw patients with fever, vomiting, nausea, body aches, and diarrhea. They degraded quickly, losing 10 percent of their bodies' fluid within twenty-four to forty-eight hours of being confirmed as having Ebola. The virus would stop their blood from clotting, and by day five or six, those affected had hemorrhagic syndrome, bleeding from their eyes and noses. The virus targets immune systems and infects their blood cells, and eventually causes multi-organ failure.

All we could do was give them potassium, IVs, pain medication, antibiotics, and Gravol and hope they would pull through. And sometimes they did.

I hadn't always wanted to be a medic. During my high school graduation party at our house, my father said he wasn't feeling well so he wished me a happy grad party, kissed me good night, and went to bed. After a few hours, my mother went to check on him and found that he wasn't breathing. I watched as my aunt, a nurse, placed him on the ground and started CPR.

We didn't have cell reception at the time, so my mother asked a friend to go farther out and call 911. To save time, we put my father in the back of a van, still doing CPR, and drove to meet up with the ambulance. He was later pronounced dead at the hospital. He had died from a heart attack at age forty-five.

I was devastated. My dad was in the military for twenty years and had inspired me to join as a military police officer, but his death changed me. I called the military and said, "I don't want to join right now. I want to become a paramedic."

I was young and inexperienced when I became a full-time city paramedic in Edmundston, New Brunswick. My dad's death was the biggest trauma I had gone through, and the whole experience tested me, made me a better medic. It made me respond better to the shootings, stabbings, and suicides I encountered on my shifts. And at the end of the day, I was so glad I wasn't an MP or a cop because I loved caring for people.

After three and a half years as a city paramedic, I had clocked 5,900 hours, but there was always a little thing inside me urging me to follow in my dad's footsteps. I wanted to travel like he did and see different cultures. So in 2006, I applied to join the army again, not as an MP, but as a medic.

I did my basic training just like everyone else, only skipping the paramedic's course because I had already done that. My first posting was to Petawawa with 2 Field Amb (Field Ambulance), and when I first got there, it was December and the regiment was training in Texas to go to Afghanistan as part of ROTO (Rotation) 6. I was eager to deploy myself and met up with my regional sergeant major to ask if I could go too. He told me I didn't have enough training, but being a young private, I was gung-ho. "This is why I joined the military," I said.

He told me I wasn't ready and to wait. In hindsight, I'm grateful that they didn't allow me to go. If they had just been looking for numbers, they could have easily brought me over, but I know I wouldn't have been ready physically or mentally. So, I waited. And trained.

In 2009, I was notified that I would be deploying with ROTO 9. It was finally my turn.

We had over a year of training for our deployment, so I felt prepared. I knew we were going into the worst case scenario. We might all die, and if we didn't, that would be a good day. Whether people got hurt with shrapnel or shot from an explosion or were severely dehydrated, it didn't shake me that bad because of everything I had already seen and experienced.

I know it sounds sappy, but I felt like my dad was my guardian angel. I remember having a good long walk and saying, "Look over me." I knew when I signed that dotted line that I could come back injured, and I was determined that I wouldn't be angry if that happened. I told myself that if I came back in one piece, I would do a half marathon. And I'm not a runner. I'm 150 pounds and all about push-ups.

While I was deployed, I never twisted my ankle or got a scratch or even gunk in my eye, and I was outside the wire every single day, sometimes doing two patrols per day. My dad was there. I came back and I did the army run in Ottawa, my first half marathon. I finished in two hours and seven minutes, and every second was amazing. I saw so many people who had been hurt and injured, and yet there they were with big smiles on their faces.

In October 2014, I was in the field doing an exercise with the brigade when my sergeant came to me and asked if I had any reason not to deploy. Did I have any issues with deploying right away? Was there someone to take care of my dog? At that time, I was long-distance with my girlfriend, now wife, so when I wasn't FaceTiming her, I was focused on staying ready. I said, "No, I'm fit. I'm good to go."

Then he asked me if I was willing to go to Sierra Leone with 2 Field Amb to treat local and international health-care workers who had been exposed to Ebola. He told me I would be part of the first rotation of Canadians to go. Again, I said yes. This was what I had signed up to do.

Within weeks, I was en route to Strensall, U.K., to undergo training with the British army's medical team who had recently come back from Sierra Leone themselves.

And I was terrified. Unlike my Afghanistan deployment, this time I felt about 30 percent prepared. I only knew what I had gleaned from Netflix, and that hadn't left a good impression. I remember seeing so many people dying and thinking, *I hope this never comes to Canada.* I had done some Googling as well, and knew that Ebola first broke out in the 1970s, but then it had gone away. Now it was back again and the pictures I saw online were horrific. What the hell had I got myself into?

Luckily, a couple of the doctors had already been to Sierra Leone and told us what to expect. In Strensall, they replicated the facility we'd be using in Sierra Leone down to a T, and we spent three weeks learning the layout, washing our hands properly to prevent Ebola contact, and donning our protective suits. By the end, I could suit up with my eyes closed.

I was very impressed with the training, and the lectures on Ebola calmed my nerves. Ebola contact was not what I thought. It's not someone who is infected spitting on your hand. It's when the saliva enters your body, and in our suits we were well protected. We just needed to follow our protocol. After our three weeks, my confidence shot up and I felt like I knew everything I possibly could.

By December, we were in Freetown, Sierra Leone.

After we landed, we jumped on a bus and started towards our facility in Kerry Town. Along the road, I began seeing signs saying "Ebola is real." And soon enough we were stopped at a checkpoint where the police took our temperatures and had us wash our hands with chlorine before continuing on.

This was the height of the Ebola crisis, and the only way to curb the disease was to teach the people how to avoid infection and to get the affected to clinics. We learned that when someone died, the custom was to clean their body and prepare them for burial within twenty-four hours, or else their soul would not go to their heaven. Unfortunately, Ebola can stay active in the body for up to seven days, so many people were getting infected just by performing these simple burial traditions. It was hard to tell a grieving family not to touch the body of their daughter or son because it was still contagious.

After seven or so more checkpoints, we arrived in Kerry Town. Our facility was exactly like the practice replica in the U.K. On the right side we had eight beds for suspected Ebola patients, those with diarrhea or a rising fever, and on the left, four beds for confirmed, those whose blood tests showed they had Ebola. Once a patient entered confirmed, they couldn't go back to suspected. They were discharged only if they had had two blood tests within forty-eight hours that confirmed they were Ebola-free.

We were quickly divided into four teams of rotating shifts so we could provide around-the-clock care. I was part of team two and paired with Emma, a nurse from Britain. One day we would work from 7 a.m. to 4 p.m., the next 4 p.m. to 11 p.m., the third day 11 p.m.

to 7 a.m., then we'd get a day off. But we were never really off. We were grabbing breakfast or sending emails home to our families and going to bed.

Each shift, Emma and I would arrive with the rest of our team and do the handover from team one. We took fifteen minutes to get a rundown of new confirmed cases or recently deceased patients. On the board, there would be updates on each patient's condition, such as "Patient in bed one is a forty-five-year-old nurse. Came in at 7 a.m. Confirmed. Currently on IV." Once we were all updated, we suited up, but not before getting our temperatures taken, which was the protocol for entering both our facility and our personal camp.

Staff used little thermometers and pointed them at our foreheads to get readings off our skin. If we had a temperature of 36 degrees (centigrade), they had to write it down. If we had a fever of 37.5, which isn't really that high, we couldn't enter the facility.

It was hot, close to 45 degrees in Sierra Leone, and we were dressing in our suits with extra layers of plastic over our chests, two masks, two pairs of gloves, and our wellies, for an average of two to three hours per shift. We would weigh ourselves before and after a shift, and some people actually lost up to seven pounds of water weight.

Because we were completely covered, our voices were muffled and the only thing our patients saw were our eyes, so we wrote our names on the plastic sheet on our chests. I wrote "Medic Lisa."

Suiting up took time, and so did moving around the facility. We had to walk slowly with our hands in front of us, our fingers intertwined, to avoid falling or touching anything we didn't need to. There was no rushing. It was the exact opposite of Afghanistan.

We had cameras and iPads set up everywhere to send videos and pictures so that if no one was in the facility, we could still monitor our patients. I had one patient who wanted to get some air outside, but he had a seizure on me. I was in my whole suit, and I couldn't lift him up because if he knocked off my visor, I would go into suspected right away. My team saw it on the camera and got two other medics to suit up and come in and help me carry him back to his bed.

Still, there were always risks, especially at night, when we were tired and the clinic was dark other than the small lamp we turned on in the room. We were dealing with IVs and needles and could easily have been exposed if we were injured with any contaminated medical equipment. We were such a tight group, because we were together for so long, that the thought of one of my friends, let alone myself, being exposed was scary.

As much as we may have wanted to rush to a patient, we couldn't. I accepted that I had to follow the safety regulations 100 percent because I knew that if I got sick, I wouldn't be able to help my patients.

———

When we arrived in December, it was the busiest time. In one shift, I would make about two trips into the facility either to change IVs, bathe someone, clean or take out garbage, or give medication. My team members would do the same, and we would rotate in and out of the facility, undressing, washing, and redressing. If we had to do three trips, we were busy.

Early on, I met Sewa. He was one of the first people I bonded with in the clinic and he had contracted Ebola. He was young and had almost finished his university courses to become a nurse.

Every second day, I would see him for maybe eight hours, and he kept getting worse and worse. He was already very slender, just bones, and Ebola was wreaking havoc on his body. He went from 120 pounds to 90 pounds. He could barely walk, and the glare of his eyes was red. Every time I saw him, I thought, *Okay, this might be the last time.* Then he'd pull through, and when I'd see him the next day, I'd think, *Okay, today might be it.*

We tried to feed him to get his weight back up and we gave him

IVs, but his fever kept rising, sometimes up to forty degrees. He was in and out of consciousness. But he would not let go.

We knew that most people died within the first forty-eight hours, so the fact that Sewa was holding on for a week was remarkable. Every time we went in, even if it was just to take the garbage out or clean an area, we would stop, take five or ten minutes, and say hi to Sewa. I remember taking the time to wash his face and hold his hand, even though mine were gloved, and he would squeeze my hand back and not let go.

Slowly, he began to make progress. And every time he did, we celebrated. "Sewa's opening his eyes!" "Oh, Sewa ate a little bit!" Every twenty-four hours, we did a blood test to confirm if he had Ebola or not. He knew he needed two good tests in a row to get discharged.

I came in one day and Sewa wasn't there. I remember asking, *What do you mean he's gone?* I found out that he had been discharged the shift before me, and while I was so glad he was well, I wish I had been there to see him walk out Ebola-free.

It was our tradition that every time a patient was discharged, they had to do an Ebola dance. Basically, they would walk out of the clinic in their pajamas and see us waiting for them, for the first time without our suits and masks on. I wished I'd gotten to see Sewa's dance.

Sierra Leone was the most satisfying experience. It was so different from Afghanistan, where anyone could get hurt at any time and things would go from zero to a hundred. I know I helped a lot of people in Afghanistan, but Sierra Leone was the highlight of my career. Every day I was sitting down and talking to my patients, helping them, which is why I joined the military in the first place. If I could, I would do that whole mission all over again in a heartbeat.

When we came back to Canada in March 2015, Ottawa was kind

of concerned about putting us in quarantine, and they did for three weeks, but at least we were home. Every day someone would call us up and make sure we didn't have temperatures. I remember they didn't want to shake our hands, which we thought was funny, given all the protocols we now knew.

Last year, I got a friend notification from Sewa on Facebook. He was trying to find all the healthcare workers who helped him in Sierra Leone. He didn't remember that I was the girl who washed his face, but he does remember me as being the Canadian medic; he remembers my eyes and the name on my jacket. He's still a nurse now in Sierra Leone.

Over the course of our rotation we took care of almost sixty people a week. We lost around half, but every month the cases were fewer and fewer. By the time the next rotation arrived, we were down to half that, and by June 2015 Sierra Leone was Ebola-free.

But it wasn't us that saved the Sierra Leone people. It was the whole population realizing that Ebola was real and that they were going to stop it. I could never take credit for stopping Ebola there because there were millions of people all over the streets taking action to prevent the further spread of the virus. They were heroes.

Master Corporal Lisa Ouellette joined the military in 2006 and has served in Afghanistan and Sierra Leone. She lives in Dartmouth, Nova Scotia, with her wife and their dog and cat.

Practicing suiting up in the Strensall, UK, facility. We weren't allowed to take pictures inside the Kerry Town clinic.

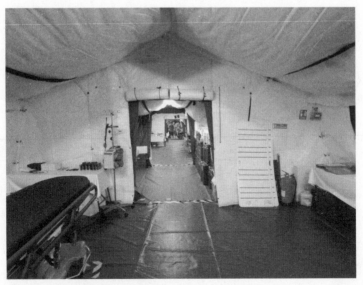

Our training facility in Strensall.

A typical checkpoint in a busy village in Sierra Leone.

I was so proud to be in Sierra Leone helping the health-care workers exposed to Ebola. This was taken on a day away from the clinic.

AFGHANISTAN

Driving Outside the Wire

Corporal Donald Hookey (Ret)

Every time we went outside the wire, we didn't
know if we were going to be hit with a roadside bomb,
a suicide bomber, or an ambush along the
side of the road.

I grew up in Port Rexton, a small Newfoundland town located on the Bonavista Peninsula, and ever since I was about twelve years old I wanted to be in the military. I had a number of relatives in both the army and air force, and I thought it was the right thing to do—to serve one's country. I was set on joining the army like my uncle, but when I went to enlist, the only open trades were those in the navy. I wanted to be a part of the Canadian Armed Forces, so I signed up anyway! I spent eleven years in the navy, then in 2004 I remustered to the army.

I left Canada for Afghanistan in January 2006 as part of the advance party for the National Support Element, whose main objective was to give full support to the battle group fighting troops. We were tasked with bringing water, fuel, rations, etc., out from the main camp of Kandahar Airfield (KAF) to the forward operating bases (FOBs). I was a mobile support equipment operator (MSE op), and it was my job to drive through the desert and mountains with supplies and ammunition all tour. As the advance party, we would also be connecting with the outgoing troops to learn the driving routes throughout the city of Kandahar and surrounding areas and the daily camp routines so that we could pass this information on to the other regiments when they finally arrived. I wasn't fully aware of what was actually going on in Afghanistan until we got on the ground, so I felt a mix of excitement and fear about the unknown path that was before me.

Within a couple of days of travelling in the heat of Afghanistan, we arrived at KAF. Just my luck, the first night there, a rocket was launched against our base. I was returning from the showers and was dressed in my shower sandals and shorts and had a towel wrapped around me when all heck broke loose. The air siren wailed and people yelled for me to run for cover. I ran and tried to get into one of the bunkers, but there was no room for me with everyone else inside. I ended up standing outside of it by myself, clutching my towel under the stars. I didn't hear an impact, so the rocket must have hit a different part of the camp. I couldn't help thinking, *What a way to start out—first day on camp and first rocket attack!*

Little did I know that by the end of the tour, we would go through such a large number of rocket attacks that we would be standing around the tent lines laughing at people scurrying like mice. We would even go a little too far once and laugh at a sergeant major tripping in his gear while on the way to the bunkers. (After that, we were told to keep our comments and laughter to ourselves, especially during a rocket attack.)

Around a third of the way through the tour, I was on an observation post (OP) with the MP attached to Bravo Company 2 PPCLI at FOB Wilson, just west of Kandahar City. I was sitting down next to the .50-caliber machine gun, a sleek black weapon with a long barrel and a range of 1 km, when a convoy approximately one mile east of our position was ambushed. Of course we all closed up on our stations and manned the main guns and our rifles.

But when others from the FOB came up to the OP I was in, a master corporal yelled out, "Who's on the fifty?"

I shouted, "It's Hookey!"

"*Who?*" he asked back.

One of the other guys that knew me said I was the trucker. Then the master corporal told me to get off the .50 and man a corner of the OP. He put one of his more experienced guys on the .50, and I went over to the corner of the OP to watch for any possible enemy activity.

But I was so drawn in by the actual fighting, I kept peering at the action instead of my arcs of fire—the designated area of responsibility I was to watch to ensure no one was firing in the wrong direction. I kept getting tapped on the helmet and told to keep my eyes peered out and not on the firefight. It was just like watching CNN when the U.S. went into Iraq in 2003. Seeing everything through the night-vision goggles made it all green with light. Tracers were flying everywhere in the distance, but mostly in the direction away from us.

The firefight lasted at least forty-five minutes before two Apache helicopters came in for air support and took over shooting up the enemy. One would circle above where they were shooting and keep lowering until they had to pull off, and then the other would do the same. They must have fired a few thousand rounds, until the convoy was able to get under way again with no major injuries.

I had just witnessed my first firefight, and a thousand thoughts were running through my mind. What would we have done if the fight had come into our arcs of fire? Would our training have taken over and won us the fight?

Meanwhile, incidents were piling up for us truckers over there in Afghanistan. Every time we went outside the wire, we didn't know if we were going to be hit with a roadside bomb, a suicide bomber, or an ambush along the side of the road. Not long into my tour, we didn't have enough truckers. We were working between eighteen and twenty hours a day, seven days a week when we were on KAF, unloading the trucks that still had stuff on them from their last run outside the wire and reloading for the next trip. We would also drive local workers around the camp and refuel the different generators, and we were often assigned to the Canadian infantry companies. We had so many assignments that supervisors who were supposed to be in the offices were actually outside the wire driving our trucks just to help out with the workload. We were busy. At the end of each day, if we weren't complaining of back pain and sore limbs, it was because we were in bed fast asleep, conked out from the never-ending labour.

In July, seven months into my tour, I was assigned to an American company, D Company (Devil Coy) of TF Warrior the 10th Mountain Division from Fort Polk, Louisiana, for Operation Mountain Thrust, which was a seek-and-destroy mission. Basically, the battle group was tasked with going out looking for Taliban fighters. I had just returned from one convoy when I was told that I would be going out on this large-scale operation with the Americans.

To be honest, I was fairly pissed off. I was hesitant to go with the Americans, as a few Canadians had already been killed in friendly fire with them that summer and I didn't want to end up as one of those statistics. I talked to one of my sergeants, told him of my concern, and he asked me if I wanted someone else to go in my place. Of course I didn't because if something were to happen to the person picked to go in my place I'd never forgive myself, so I went. But not before asking the sergeant to pass a message to my wife just in case something was to happen to me. I told him to tell her that she was an excellent mother, that I was sorry I never made it home, and that I loved her and the girls.

I was told to ensure the truck was loaded and ready to go, so we off-loaded what was on the back of the truck and reloaded what we needed for the Americans. Water, rations, and fuel. This took at least an hour, as we had to stack everything on pallets and board them in to prevent any fuel spillage from ruining the water or rations.

I had no clue where the Americans were, so I went to the rally point to find out if anyone knew where the company had staged before the big road move through the city. No one had seen them, so I went back to our compound to see if my supervisors had any other information on a possible contact. I was told that the American company had left the rally point over two hours earlier and that I was just a corporal with few qualifications, so I had to get my ass out to them somehow! That was hard to hear, but honestly I was expendable. Any other trucker back in Canada could replace me if something were to happen, but I had chosen to serve my country, I was there in Afghanistan, and I had a job to do.

The only way I knew how to find the Americans was to beg my way onto another convoy. So I asked a sergeant that I knew if my co-driver and I could tag along with him. He agreed, and we stopped at every convoy and compound in Kandahar City and asked if anyone had seen Devil Coy. It was the same answer at every stop until the final one of the day. I saw an infantry warrant officer that had been attached to Devil Coy earlier in the tour, and he told me that the only Americans he knew of were the ones over to the right of his position. He said if that wasn't Devil Coy, we could stay with his company until the end of the operation.

But it was! And they were extremely surprised to see us, especially once I said that we had their supplies for the operation. Until we showed up, they had been trying to figure out how they were going to get resupplied. A lieutenant took me directly over to the Headquarters Platoon and introduced me to the executive officer and the captain. My co-driver and I felt like royalty.

The next morning we moved to the northern part of Helmand Province searching for Taliban fighters. We were stationary for a day or so and had parked our circle of vehicles not too far from a village just over a ridge. One night, my co-driver and I were on the .50-cal watch from the American first sergeant's vehicle, and we saw these strange shadows moving across the ground through the night-vision scope on the .50. The depth perception was much better than that of night-vision goggles, and it looked like these shadows were a group of animals with long tails crawling around, maybe some kind of rat. The following day, we saw holes burrowed into the ground big enough for someone's foot to get caught in. I asked the first seargent what they were, but he didn't know; he just compared them to prairie dogs. I decided right then and there that I wasn't sleeping on the ground anymore, just in case one of these animals dragged me away. From then on, we slept on top of our cargo in the back of the truck.

Another day during the operation, one of the interpreters wandered off for a walk not too far from where we were. When he returned, he came right to the Headquarters Platoon and showed us a cylinder that he found just lodged in the ground. It had a digital face with numbers on it and was about twelve inches long. When the first seargent saw it, he immediately told the interpreter to follow him over to the EOD (explosive ordnance disposal) techs. They suited up and took the cylinder about three hundred to four hundred metres away from all of the company, then detonated it with explosives. I managed to get a photo of the actual explosion. There was a loud boom, but the flash wasn't overly big, and there were no flames. It wasn't like those great big Hollywood movie explosions. After that the interpreter was told if he found anything else on the ground to just leave it and come tell someone where it was located instead of endangering all the lives of the company.

We continued to travel the desert in search of Taliban, but it wasn't until mid-July, close to the end of Operation Mountain Thrust, that we came across some fighters. At this point in the operation, four different Humvees had broken down, and I had towed them out to the main road so the recovery team from KAF could come get them. One of them was the mortar platoon vehicle, which carried the mortar platoon and the ammunition. Just like that, my co-driver and I became the supply, recovery, and mortar platoon vehicles.

The Americans sent out a small patrol to do a little recce on a village just over the ridge from where we were stationed. They came under some pretty heavy fire and the vehicle that took the majority of hits managed to make it back to us. I could see the Humvee had its hood all shot up full of bullet holes. Just then an order was given to move towards the fighting, and there was no time to think. We picked up everything and went into the firefight full tilt.

We got to the top of the ridge and unloaded the mortars so the team could use them for suppressive fire on the enemy. As gunfire echoed around us, we began searching our surroundings. There was a small compound with about four mud huts to our direct right about 250 metres away from us. The executive officer of the company yelled out to me, my co-driver, his mechanic, and one of the interpreters to follow him to help clear the compound. To this day, I don't know how that man could run like he did and still bark out orders to us. I was sucking wind through every orifice of my body.

He sent me to the top of one of the mud huts to keep a watchful eye on the entire compound while the interpreter and mechanic took the right side of the compound and he and my co-driver took the left side. I climbed up to the top of the mud hut by jumping and hauling myself on top of it. By this time I was already sweating, dirty, and breathing heavily. The only thing going through my mind at the time was to ensure my eyes were scanning the compound looking for any potential threats. Minutes after my team left, two Afghani men came walking out of the centre of the compound. I told them to stop and put their hands on their heads. Even though this wasn't the first time that I had to confront someone in Afghanistan, all I thought was, *I sure hope they don't have weapons.* They complied and I jumped down from my position on top of the mud hut and moved closer, covering their every move.

Once the others returned to the centre of the compound, I was ordered to go and investigate the mud-hut doors that hadn't been checked yet. I ended up kicking in the door to the barn and got a start from the cow that was in there. (My co-driver told me later that when he kicked in his first door, a chicken jumped into his face! He nearly pissed himself.) Once the compound was cleared of possible weapons, we let the Afghanis go.

After we moved back to the ridge, my co-driver went off with the American infantry and I stayed back with the mortar team in case they needed help. There was a large amount of radio traffic during this firefight, and the CO of the Canadian battle group had also come in to help.

As the firefight went on, they called in for mortar support, but it was "Danger Close," which meant the mortars would be close to the enemy but also close to our own troops. Before the mortars could be fired, the team had to reposition them twice to get a good spot, to be on the same grid as those close to the enemy. I offered to help and they asked if I had ever fired a mortar round before. Of course my answer was no, but they were down men from the mortar platoon so they agreed to let me fire the rounds. Thus began my major crash course on how to prep and fire the mortars. We were using M252 81mm mortars, so we were programming them to explode either just above the ground (an air burst), when they hit the ground, or after a delay. There were only about twenty mortar rounds, and we fired between twelve and fifteen. It didn't take long for the Taliban to tuck tail and run when the rounds were landing right on top of their position.

After the firefight we went and searched the area for dead or wounded. We found some blood, but the Taliban had removed their casualties, just as we would have done. By then, it was getting dark so we pushed back to our original position in the middle of the desert and bunked down for the night. It didn't hit me until later, when I was settling in, that any of us could have been injured or even killed at any moment during that firefight.

Over the next couple of days we went to the southern part of Helmand Province, to where the Taliban had run the Afghan National Police (ANP) out of another compound that housed a school and a hospital. The Taliban had burned out the two places, and we showed up to take the compound back. But to our surprise we didn't have any resistance. After a few more days we were set loose to go back to KAF on our own accord because the operation was pretty much over. Nothing happened on our long trip back to KAF, so we had a lot of time to think and chat about what we'd been through during Operation Mountain Thrust.

The remainder of my tour I went back outside the wire a few more times on different convoys without any major incidents of my own, but there were a few other truckers who had really close calls with suicide bombers. I can't count how many times I could have lost my life over in Afghanistan. I still have nightmares about some of the things I've seen.

I'm now home in Newfoundland, but looking back at my time in Afghanistan I can honestly say that even though we really didn't have enough personnel over there, we still managed to do everything that was thrown our way. Sometimes we weren't trained to do the things that were asked of us, and we had to adapt and overcome many challenges. For the most part, we did our jobs with a smile and a chuckle. I was so relieved to return to Canada and see my family, but to this day, I still have the feeling of unfinished business, that we could have done even more in Afghanistan. I would go back in a heartbeat if I could.

Corporal Donald Hookey (Ret) joined the navy in 1993 and served as a radio operator on the HMCS *Provider*, the HMCS *Preserver*, and the HMCS *Charlottetown*. On the *Preserver*, he was part of the recovery operation of Swissair Flight 111 that crashed off Peggy's Cove, Nova Scotia, on September 2, 1998. He also toured the Persian Gulf on the *Charlottetown* before remustering into the army in 2004. In 2006, he deployed to Afghanistan with 1 Service Battalion as part of the National Support Element. Donald currently lives in Conception Bay South, Newfoundland, with his wife and two daughters. He volunteers with VETS (Veterans Emergency Transition Services) Canada as the field operations manager for Newfoundland and Labrador.

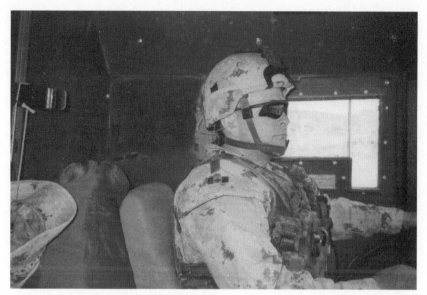

Around the beginning of the tour, in an HLVW (Heavy Logistic Vehicle Wheeled), a ten-ton, six-wheeled truck, on our way to a platoon house called Gumbad. We always wore earplugs to help prevent concussions in case we hit an IED.

Outside the wire, getting ready to fire mortars at the Taliban.

Wearing the Maple Leaf

Leading Seaman Bruno Guévremont (Ret)

*When there is a risk of life, our operating procedure
is to go in bare ass. We don't send the robots, we don't
put on bomb suits, we just move.*

I grew up in Gatineau, Quebec, and I joined the army in July of 1999.
As a kid, I was lucky to travel a lot, and when I was ten years old, I
lived in Zaire, Africa, for a year. That experience opened up my eyes
about the world, and I realized that we have a great country, a beautiful place to live, so I grew up with a calling to serve. It seemed very
natural to join the military.

The whole time I was in training I had one goal in mind—to be
a paratrooper. I wanted to jump out of planes! But first, I had to go
through basic, then train for my trade. After that, I was posted to
2 Service Battalion in Petawawa as a weapons technician, and daily,
I would ask our NCO if I could go on the jump course. He would
always respond, "No, it's not going to happen."

At the time, it was hard for a trade person like me, someone who
fixed weapons, to get paratrooper training because those courses were
reserved for those in infantry or combat. But in the wake of 9/11, the

PPCLI was deployed to Afghanistan, and just like that, spots freed up on the jump course. I got my chance.

I soon discovered that there's nothing natural about jumping out of a plane. It's the scariest and yet most exhilarating thing at the same time. There I was surrounded by a great bunch of guys all with the same objective as me—to jump.

After passing the jump course, I went on to complete my qualifying whole trade course, and from there was posted to 3 RCR. They had a para company, but jump positions were paid and reserved for the guys who did the fighting. Luckily, the company realized that they needed a weapons tech and two vehicle techs to go with them on deployments, so they reopened those three maintenance positions. I got a spot and was the last weapons tech in Canada to wear a maroon beret, which is given only to jump-qualified personnel. I had been told no about two hundred times, and finally I was living my dream.

Not too long after that, we got our first deployment to Afghanistan. When I heard the news, I felt no hesitation—this is what I had signed up for.

We would be the first rotation of Canadian troops for Task Force Kabul, Operation Athena. We landed mid-July 2003 and for six months were stationed out of Kabul as part of ISAF (International Security Assistance Force), a NATO mission to ensure a safe environment while the political leaders of Afghanistan developed their constitution. ISAF was very organized and fairly tame despite what some might think. Once we set up camp, we started doing patrols. ROTO 0 was a pretty good eye-opener to Afghanistan. There weren't any close calls until near the end, when we lost two men in a roadside blast. That was hard to take.

—————

When I came back in early 2004, there was a lot of downtime at 3 RCR in Petawawa, so I began researching something more exciting to do—

how to become a clearance diver. I'd heard of this small, elite group of highly skilled divers whose primary job was underwater explosives and demolitions. Some might call me an adrenaline junkie, but I think I'm absolutely normal. Clearance diver is almost an unknown trade (there are only 120 of them across Canada), and there were a lot of hoops I had to jump through before even being considered for training. I didn't know if I would make it, but I had to try.

I remustered to the navy and became a boatswain (shortest trade course) on the HMCS *Regina* so that I could apply for diving courses. But before I could, I was deployed on a goodwill tour in East Asia. We travelled to Japan, Korea, China, and Hawaii, and our CO met with dignitaries from each country. I soon found out that there's a big difference between where you can go in the navy versus the army. On our tour, I made a deal with the chief that if I had a good deployment, when we returned, I'd be put on the ship's team diver course. He agreed, and once the *Regina* returned to port, I started my six weeks with the fleet diving unit.

We learned how to take mines off the ship's hull, how to detangle ropes in the propellers, and other maintenance. It was probably one of the best courses I've ever done. It was intense and made us extremely physically fit. At the end, I knew I would either be recommended to go on selection for clearance diver or go back to my ship and continue with my boatswain trade. As luck would have it, I was recommended. The pieces were falling into place. All I had to do was ace a gruelling ten-day course to be selected for my clearance diving. We started with thirty and finished with eight, including me. Just three years after I'd returned from Afghanistan, I started the training to become a clearance diver. It was finally happening.

About five months in, while we were doing a standard dive, I got decompression sickness. The docs thought I had blown one of my lungs. I was taken off the course for obvious safety reasons, but I recovered well, and the fleet diving unit wanted to bring me back. The higher-ups really liked me so they sent me on a counter-IED course, which is usually re-served for fully qualified clearance divers who have had lots of training.

But even after I completed the explosives course, the medical team still didn't want me to dive because I was at risk for blowing my lung. If I did, it wouldn't repair itself the way it was supposed to and any pressure would cause further injury.

Meanwhile, the Royal 22nd Regiment was preparing to deploy to Afghanistan, but one of the counter-IED operators on the bomb-disposal team couldn't go because of personal problems. They were about a month from deployment, and they needed someone who was counter-IED qualified and who had already been to Afghanistan. Me.

At lunch one day in February my CO pulled me into his office and asked if I wanted to go.

Right away, I said yes.

I had gotten married before coming to the navy and had recently had my first son, so my CO mentioned that I might want to talk to my wife before giving my answer.

I said, "Sir, I signed up to do these things, but I'll go talk to her. She knows this is what we do."

He suggested I leave then and make sure it was okay. My wife was really surprised to see me home in the middle of the day. I told her the news that I'd be leaving in a month and we made it work.

April 2009, my unit had boots on the ground in Kandahar. We had five days of indoctrination, as they call it, five days to get our kits and head out to our FOB, Camp Nathan Smith.

Three hours into our first day at Camp Nathan Smith, we got our first call. And so began the busiest six months of my life.

When we arrived on scene, we saw that three suicide bombers had detonated in a market in front of the governor's house. The area was total carnage. Nothing like what I had encountered on my first tour. We proceeded to conduct a safety check, then we carried out a post-blast investigation—how many bombers, what the bombs were, where they detonated, and how much damage was caused. We collected samples and sent them back to the network that re-creates evidence.

After that first day, the calls never stopped. We got anywhere between two to three a day, and one day we got nine. We would leave the gate in the morning with a call, and by the time we got to that first call, we'd have two more. Over the whole campaign, our team answered over one hundred calls. There was no stopping. To stay calm and focused, in between calls I would listen to Norah Jones.

Now, the intel we'd get wasn't always accurate. One time we were told we had two rockets under a bridge, and we followed the Afghan police to a place with no bridge and no rockets, and we were actually right in the middle of a minefield. We never knew what we were getting into.

We were a small team of five men and we had two operators. We always switched operators between calls. We weren't superstitious, but was just bad juju to break the system. What if you go down range when it's not your turn and something happens? What if someone goes downrange for you and something happens?

One day in June 2009, we received a call about a suicide bomber, and up until that point, anytime we would get a call about a suicide bomber, they would have already detonated or someone would have shot them and they'd be dead by the time we got there. So we had kind of a relaxed response when these kinds of calls came in.

I was the operator on this particular call, so when we arrived, I dismounted and went over to our ANP contact with our translator. To reduce risk, no one else dismounts, but for some reason, our team did that day.

Through the translator, I asked the ANP guy what was going on.

"We're looking for the suicide bomber," he replied.

"What do you mean you're looking for him? Where is he?"

"We don't know! He was running around."

"What? He's alive?"

Throughout the whole tour, we always had intel that we were the big target, that we were being filmed, followed, etc., because the Taliban were looking for ways to beat us. As bomb techs, we put a wrench in their plans.

Immediately I said, "Everybody, back in your vehicles. The bomber is running around."

As soon as we were back in, we got a call saying they found him, which I assumed meant that they shot him. My alert level came way back down. In my head I was thinking that I would go to the location, take the bomb off him with the robot, and we'd be good to go. When you went to a call, you created a scenario in your head so you could deal with each incident calmly.

I went to the intersection of the road where they said the bomber was, and I saw two guys holding another man by his arms a little ways off. The chief of the Afghan Secret Police was also there. I'd met him a couple of times, and he was very distinguished, smart, and composed. He always reminded me of Hani Salaam, the Jordanian intelligence operative played by Mark Strong in *Body of Lies*.

The chief and I made the proper introduction—*As-salāmu 'alaykum*—and we shook hands. Through the translator he said, "We had intel that this guy was coming to kill President Karzai's half-brother. He was waiting for him to detonate."

I looked over at the man, and I could see that he was wearing a vest and had two switches hanging from his hands. We were worried he was going to detonate right there. We gave the two men holding him some zap straps and we secured the man to a fence nearby. After that I pushed everyone back and went to work.

When there is a risk of life, our operating procedure is to go in bare ass. We don't send the robots, we don't put on bomb suits, we just move. The Canadian Forces are some of the best trained forces in the world. I was so focused on what I was doing, I never feared for my life. I was stone-cold. I went in with my roll of duct tape, scissors, and some wire cutters.

As I approached the bomber, I felt like I was walking into a six-by-six-foot hot box of energy. It was like I stepped into a sauna, like an oven door just opened in front of me. I'd never experienced that before.

I looked at the device he was wearing and followed the wiring to see how it was made because there's more than one way to detonate a suicide vest. "Victim-operated" means that the suicide bomber detonates the switch. "Anti-removal" means if he takes it off, it blows up. And then there's the "chicken switch," which means someone remotely detonates it in case the suicide bomber gets shot. At this close proximity, there was nothing a bomb suit would have done to protect me anyway.

I studied the vest's wiring and circuits, and I knew it wasn't an anti-removal device, so I began taking it off him. Once I did, he let out a big sigh of relief and he said something in Afghan, which I didn't understand. That's when the hot box disappeared. I knew this was a victim-operated device, so I walked away from the guy into the middle of the street and completely dismantled the vest and rendered it safe, so the rest of the bomb tech team could conduct the investigation.

I was told that was the first time in Canadian Forces history that someone had taken a vest off a live suicide bomber. And because he survived, we were able to interrogate him. We discovered that the bomber was mentally challenged, that he had been starved for two weeks and been told that if he didn't do this, his family would be killed. I felt so sorry for him. I could see in his face that he didn't want any part of the Taliban. That information gave me a whole new perspective on war; it put a face to it and I no longer thought of everyone with a suicide vest as a bad guy.

Between six to nine months after I got back, I noticed that I was reacting differently to things. When I was working, I was completely focused on whatever I was doing: jumping, diving, and dismantling bombs. I never experienced anxiety, panic attacks, or depression, so when those feelings came around, I wasn't sure how to respond. I began getting angry really quickly. I had a short temper. If I smelled diesel, I would immediately be overseas again. I started having flashbacks and nightmares.

I went to see our Forces doctor, Christina, who suggested I might be struggling with PTSD.

There was no way. I said, "Doc, I don't know where you went to school, but I don't get PTSD."

I had my wife and my amazing son. Being a dad was so important to me, but I was suffering. I wasn't sleeping or eating. I wasn't doing anything good. One day, I made a plan and I decided I was going to end my life.

Before I did, I went to Christina one more time and told her what I was prepared to do.

"I have a plan, and this is the location and how I'm going to do it. What do we do now?" I asked her for help.

She was all in. She sent me to the Mental Health Clinic and they got me on medication. The military system was extremely good at helping me get back on my feet. I was diagnosed with PTSD and was no longer deployable, so the Canadian Forces made the decision to medically release me. That was one of the hardest things to accept. I had been in the military for fifteen years, and it was who I was. I had to reinvent myself.

———

In 2014, I connected with business leaders on an expedition to the North Pole through the True Patriot Love Foundation. They mentored me and I opened my own gym, where I have the opportunity to help others. The first thing I tell them is that they're not alone and that they don't have to suffer in silence.

One of the first things you learn in basic training is to suffer in silence. It's part of the process of breaking you down and building you back up as a team. One NCO will tell you to get on the bus, then another NCO will ask you what you're doing and tell you to get off. It can get chaotic. If you speak up, they say, "Are you talking back to me?" Then they put you in the push-up position and you start doing push-ups. From day one of basic, no one is in good shape, so everyone groans and moans, "Oh my god, I can't do this anymore." And the NCO says, "Shut up, suffer in silence." And you hear that throughout your career.

We're trained not to speak up when we're battling something. Now, being on the other side, I tell people, if you talk about it, you can do something about it. It doesn't mean you're less of a warrior, or that you're weak. You're actually stronger, and by voicing your struggle, you're liberating others to do the same. Every time we tell our stories, we heal a bit more.

In 2016, I was asked to be the team captain for Canada at the Invictus Games and recruit thirty athletes. I said yes, of course, but I remember thinking, *How the hell am I going to take care of thirty ill and injured athletes, when I don't even have my shit together?*

The Invictus Games are all about helping people get back on their feet. There were about five members on the team who were ready to call it quits, and having an international competition like Invictus in their sights turned things around for them. They started training like athletes, their health got better, their family lives improved because they were part of a team once more. And not only that, they were wearing the maple leaf on their shoulders again. For us, that's the most important thing.

Leading Seaman Bruno Guévremont (Ret) was born in Gatineau, Quebec, and in 1999 joined the Canadian Army, where he trained as a weapons technician. He has completed two tours in Afghanistan, and on the second, he worked on an elite squad of bomb technicians (C-IED). Bruno is the only Canadian to have successfully disarmed a live suicide bomber. In 2016, he was named captain of Team Canada at the Invictus Games in Orlando, Florida. Bruno has turned fitness into a form of therapy, opening his own gym, CrossFit Stasis, in Victoria, B.C., where he offers fitness and life coaching to everyone, including veterans and military and emergency services personnel. In 2017, he was honoured to be named an ambassador of the Bell Let's Talk campaign.

We would often find IEDs in the ground and detonate them. Here I am setting the timer on my watch before activating the fuse.

Digging up a booby-trapped wire that had injured a fellow Canadian. It led to four well-placed IEDs that we disarmed.

In my bomb suit, geared out to go downrange and set up a hook and line to disrupt an IED.

It'll Make a Man Out of You

CORPORAL ANDY GILL

You can mentally prepare for Afghanistan, you can train and shoot at targets, but nothing will prepare you to be in constant danger, to be actively engaging with other human beings on the other end of that gun.

I was just out of university and feeling kind of directionless, but my grandfather had high hopes for me and suggested that I join the military. An ex-military man himself, he said, "It'll make a man out of you."

I guess it was in my bloodline. My grandfather had been an officer in the intelligence corps, and I had so much respect for the things he had done and the lives he had helped. I'm sure I inherited this from him, but the ultimate draw to join the military was this innate desire to help those in need—the children, women, and men who were helplessly implicated in a war that reached far beyond their doors.

So I joined on September 30, 2006, as a reservist with the 1 Military Police Regiment in Richmond, British Columbia. Despite my grandfather's support, the rest of my family was not as keen for me to enlist. My mom was adamantly against it; she just said, "You're not going.

Absolutely not." My dad was a little more understanding. He and my siblings were apprehensive, but they were willing to support me. I was a member of the Forces only on a volunteer basis.

Around Christmas of 2007, shortly after finishing my basic training and qualifications, I got the call. It was as simple as "Hey, a spot opened up if you want it." And that was it. To be honest, I didn't really think I would be deployed. But then I got the call, and I figured it was a good idea. I wasn't doing anything else with my life. My grandfather was originally from Pakistan, and my family is of Indian descent, so I thought it would be a good opportunity to travel there and explore those roots.

Next thing I knew, I was flying to Edmonton for pre-deployment training in February of 2008. It was a new adventure, and I was excited. We spent eight months doing various exercises in Wainwright, Alberta, and by September, our rotation started flying into Kandahar. I was one of the first ones to fly over on our rotation, and I had only just found out that I would be on the Operational Mentoring and Liaison Team, otherwise known as OMLT—yes, it sounds like the eggs. We waited around in Kandahar Airfield for a couple of days, and then I got ripped out on a chopper to somewhere in the Zhari district with my team.

When I first got there, boots on the ground, I was inside the wire and I felt relatively safe. But after three days of being in theatre, the minute I jumped into the back of that vehicle, it was real. I had gone beyond those gates, and I was in the heart of Afghanistan. On that first road move in Zhari, the whole time I was thinking, *Please don't get blown up, please don't get blown up.* Because you hear about that. I was on edge for that entire drive. But we made it safely, and from then on, it was about establishing routine.

As an OMLT member, our job was to live with the local ANP. We were there to build rapport with the locals and provide security for the area, but also to teach the ANP how to police their area. Nothing was ever quite up to Canadian standards, but we learned to adapt to our new environment very quickly. We had to adapt our policing techniques, but we also had to adapt to the culture.

Between my grandfather and our pre-deployment training, I knew the way of life there, what you could get away with and what you couldn't—the dos and don'ts. It was as simple as don't talk to or look at the women, but do talk to the village elders. But then again, because we were foreigners, we didn't always get what we wanted; we couldn't just impose our will on them. I think that was a big shock to the Westerners in Afghanistan. We had to relearn how to show our respect to the Afghan people. For example, if you were invited into their homes for a cup of tea, you accepted the invitation. To reject it was to disrespect them. The ANP would often share cups of tea or meals with us, and I always obliged because I had to earn their respect. Not all the guys I was with understood that. You could see the walls build up as soon as they declined them.

The police mentoring team was fully embedded in the Afghan lifestyle. We didn't have the luxury of living in the FOBs like the kaffers or fobbits—those who never left KAF or FOBs. While they were working out, drinking Tim Hortons, and eating their Burger King, we were rotating through ANP substations for three or four nights at a time, only taking a break one night in between to refuel and sleep before heading back out to another substation.

We lived out of the substations with the Afghans, and together we would patrol the areas of responsibility that we were assigned. When we weren't patrolling, we'd teach the ANP how to do vehicle checkpoints, how to maintain security, and how to engage with the locals. We'd do range days with them and teach them how to shoot. We'd teach first-aid training, so that if they were out shopping in the market, they could actually bandage their buddies up if they needed to. They were receptive to that stuff; it was nice to see that they were learning.

In many of the villages, among the elders and the tribes, somebody was always related to somebody, so it was difficult to successfully establish security for the Afghan people in the area. Once we were set up, we'd often find that a farmer was using the area to grow crops, and of course the biggest exports were opium and marijuana. That's just how they made money. The reality, though, is that many of those men had multiple kids and wives at home, and they were trying to support their families. So if we started clearing out brush, their crops, the farmers would no longer be able to feed their families. I don't think anybody could have anticipated that we'd run into those kinds of problems.

The whole idea and principle was to work with the locals, to hopefully push the Taliban out of the area, but corruption among the ANP was not uncommon. They could be imbedded with the Taliban, be paid off, or their families could be threatened. We had to get to a point where we could build that relationship with them, to work together. It was a challenge. When you're in a firefight, you have to trust the guy next to you, whether he is ANP, an American, or a fellow Canadian.

———————

A couple of weeks into my tour, just after my birthday, I heard a snap and a crack—the first sounds of the firefight. I didn't really know what it would sound like, but I heard that snap and crack, and saw the dirt spew out by my legs, and it was like a light went on in my head. There was no question, *Holy fuck, we're in this now.*

It was complete and utter chaos. I couldn't hear anything except for the *snap, crack, snap, crack* of the bullets whizzing by my head. I was engaged, but I couldn't see where the shots were coming from. We knew they were close, probably about two hundred metres away, but with the density of the terrain, we didn't have good sightlines on them. As a member of the OMLT, in the midst of the firefight I was also teaching the ANP how to shoot more effectively. I had to watch them to make sure they were following directions, but also to make sure they didn't turn on me. It was a balancing act. I was so focused on what I was doing that I felt numb to what was happening around me.

But the rounds were coming right at me, and I realized that if didn't find cover right away, I'd get shot. So I dove into a wadi, the closest cover I could find. A wadi is essentially a ditch of water, where people take a piss and shit. It may not sound like the best idea, but considering my circumstances, I had no other choice. I don't know how long I was in the wadi before I pulled myself out and started peeling out of the area. Time has a funny way of stopping in moments like that. But we eventually disengaged, and by the time we got back to the FOB, we were soaked, drenched in sweat. That was just the beginning.

I learned pretty quickly that we were sitting ducks. I would talk to the locals once we were settled at a police substation, and they would say the things I wanted to hear, but we weren't really getting through to them. I would let them know that we were there to provide security and I'd ask them what they needed. But shortly after establishing ourselves in a village, we'd be getting shot at from within that same village.

You can mentally prepare for Afghanistan, you can train and shoot at targets, but nothing will prepare you to be in constant danger, to be actively engaging with other human beings on the other end of that gun. Yeah, somebody is trying to kill you, but you don't have time in that moment to realize those things. Somebody shoots at you, and you shoot back. You're always in danger; it's just the environment.

One night, we were sitting in our police substation, and the rule was that at nighttime, somebody was always up. I was watching our arcs of fire and security around our substation and saw some of the Afghans leaving the compound without even telling us. But obviously we could still see them on the thermal image, walking out with their AK-47s. They were standing fifty metres outside our compound smoking hash. They were supposed to be going out for a patrol in about two hours, and they were doing hash. It was frustrating to say the least.

I remember going out for patrols, and I'd be so afraid to even walk. Explosive devices were so common there, I would just be walking, thinking, *I do not want these things going off.* There would be times when I'd stop walking and stand there, convinced that if I moved I'd get blown up, because I thought there was something underneath me.

We had our ECMs (electronic countermeasures), but we could have had all the technology in the world, and I still wouldn't have been prepared. I was there to do a job, and there was nothing I could do about it. I just hoped that the guys and girls around me got home safely.

Of course, there were a lot of good guys in the ANP. I remember this one guy in particular—I actually keep his picture on my computer, and every time I look at it, it makes me smile. He was a good guy. He was from northern Afghanistan, and he'd left his family, all six kids, to make his country better. I found out later that he ended up dying. But he was always right next to me on patrol, because I knew I could trust him. He was there to make changes, and he was right there with us in a firefight. The team as a whole was not bad. We would share meals together. We may not have spoken the same language, but there was a common bond that held us together, and I was in awe of some of them. They left their families and everything else behind, sacrificed so much, just to make things better for their country.

When you can put a name and a face to the loss, it really humanizes things. That may seem obvious, but amid the shooting, you don't have time to feel anything. We lost one of our men. He was one of my lieutenants and had a wife and a kid back in Saskatchewan. We had been on the same team during work-up training and I remember a conversation I had with him. He told me he had a problem with people getting beaten, that he thought somebody had to do something about it. We were both going overseas for the same reason. We both wanted to help the helpless, and we bonded over that desire, despite the difference in rank. I remember the day we found out that he'd died. Everything shut down; it was radio silence. It's hard to describe that loss, because the camaraderie among the Canadian military is like no other. It's home.

There were Afghan losses too that I've never been able to forget. My team was under attack at a police substation, and we ended up in a firefight. We called in a helicopter and they launched hellfire missiles at the Taliban, then we made our way back to our FOB because some of our guys had injuries and we had to get them to medical. On my way through the FOB front gates, I saw this man pushing a wheelbarrow. I thought, *What the hell does he have in that wheelbarrow?* When I approached him, I saw that he had two bodies, two little kids, in the wheelbarrow. He looked at me, and I looked at him, and I was lost for words. What did he expect me to say to him? I don't know what happened to that little girl and boy, but their images haunt me. To this day, I still can't escape them. We never could pinpoint what happened to them, but I worry about it. Were they dead from one of our missiles? I don't know for sure, but the idea screwed with my head. I hated the FOB after that. I hated going back there.

When I think about it now, that incident was my turning point. I had enlisted to help the children who were helplessly thrown into a war, and there I was, watching two young children literally being carted away. It wasn't easy coming back to Canada after seeing the things I saw in Afghanistan. It's not a simple adjustment to come back and be expected to function, to pay a mortgage, to have friends. I didn't have a support system until I met my wife, and I don't know what I'd do without her. She came out of nowhere, and I am so grateful for her. She just lets me be. She's patient. She lets me have my bad days, and then asks, "Okay, what do you need?"

I did settle into a new routine in Canada. I have a professional career and still serve with the reserves. I miss Afghanistan, the people, and, as crazy as it sounds, the firefights; I miss the gunfights. I often think about what my grandfather taught me when I was younger: if you don't stand up for what's right, then who the hell is going to? He isn't alive today, but sometimes I sit here and think of him, and I know what he meant when he said the military would make a man out of me.

Corporal Andy Gill joined the army in 2006 and served in Afghanistan from 2009 to 2010. He lives a quiet life with his wife and daughter in the Lower Mainland of British Columbia.

These were the living quarters for our team at a police substation in Pashmul, Zhari district. The tent at the front on the right is mine.

In a tower at another police substation, keeping watch.

One of my friends in the ANP. We took a candid photo together after a patrol.

Leading the Valiant Troops of 2 RCR

Lieutenant Colonel David Quick (Ret)

As the months went by in theatre, my anxiety grew
because I knew from a mathematics perspective that
I would soon lose soldiers. . . . Every time we went out
on a mission, I felt that worry, but death didn't come.

I'd like to tell you that I was brought up thinking I would become a great warrior, but no, I joined the military as plan B. I grew up in Trenton, Ontario, which is an air force base town, and for a while, I thought I'd like to become a pilot, like in *Top Gun*. But I am colourblind and I didn't have the greatest grades, so I ended up at Guelph University, drinking my tuition money away, to be honest. In 1994, I needed a job.

I joined what's called the Officer Candidate Training Program, essentially a program that allows you to be commissioned without a university degree. If I completed the infantry officer training successfully, I would be commissioned as an officer (read: have a job), but if I failed, I'd go back to school. So I went through the "grinder" and came out the other side after about a year of consecutive leadership and infantry courses.

I was posted to 1 RCR in Petawawa in 1995, and for the first couple of years in the army, it still felt like plan B for me. I hadn't drunk the Kool-Aid yet. I loved my friends in the unit, but in the nineties I was questioning everything, including the military culture. I was just a kid, twenty-one years old, with a brain that was still forming. But we had some key leaders at that time that changed my philosophy. One was Jim Davis, my first company commander. He was like a big brother to me, and over the years he became one of my mentors. But it wasn't until I went to Bosnia in 1998 that I started to fall in love with the army. It felt really good to be a Canadian there, helping the way we were.

While in 1 RCR, I did all the classic young-officer jobs: rifle platoon commander, reconnaissance platoon commander, second in command of a company. I learned a lot, and every role was focused on spending time with the soldiers and perfecting my craft. I was the young, uneducated guy coming in, the same age as them, and I think we bonded. In many ways I had more in common with the soldiers at that time than I did with my brother and sister officers. I still wanted to finish school so I could get a "real job" in case my military career didn't work out, so while at Petawawa I continued to work on my unfinished undergrad degree on my own time through distance education.

I deployed to Kosovo in 1999 with 1 RCR and upon my return was posted to my first headquarters job in Toronto, where I worked for both Generals Gauthier and Leslie. In my aide-de-camp role I learned another side of the army and watched a very different leadership style than what I had previously been exposed to. During this time I mentioned to General Gauthier and General Leslie that I'd like to finish my schooling, and they kindly supported my return to full-time studies (for one year) to complete my undergrad degree through the Army Officer Degree Program. After that, I was sent to Army Staff College (pre-major school) and then back to the battalion.

My life really began to change when I was posted to 2 RCR in 2003 and promoted from an operations officer to company commander. My career was taking off. After a fascinating rapid deployment to Haiti in 2004 under Jim Davis's command, I was honoured to take command of India Company in 2 RCR. In 2006, I was notified that we would be deploying to Afghanistan the next January. I was thirty-three.

We landed in the Zhari district a few months after the infamous Operation Medusa, the historic battle with 1 RCR in the birthplace of the Taliban. We felt that we inherited the most critical battle space. But it was winter, and the area looked almost like a mix between southern Ontario and a George Lucas film set. The cold meant people were inside staying warm, not out fighting.

Needless to say, we had almost a false sense of security as we moved around. We thought, *We're young, spry. What's the big deal?* I would later eat those thoughts as they were baked into several pieces of humble pie! I had only ever trained for combat, so I was learning what we should be doing "on the job." We spent a couple of months patrolling, studying the ground and the communities, trying to keep our game faces on. In hindsight, we were experiencing a lull that we would not fully appreciate until spring arrived and the fighting season commenced.

By spring, my group was very intimate with our AOR in the Zhari district. We had walked so much of the insurgents' ground, knew where the trails and bridges and every nook and cranny were. That piece of land was like our own backyard, and that knowledge became a key to much of our success. The infantry is all about the intimacy with where you must function—knowing the ground so you can hold it or seize it.

From April to August, the tempo picked up and almost every ninety-six hours my team was on a deliberate operation. Not troops-in-contact (TIC), where you stumble into a firefight or an ambush, but a deliberately planned mission with objectives. We carried out twenty-four named operations, where we had formal orders and rehearsals before heading out, and those were outside of the day-to-day TICs that occurred at the platoon level. My soldiers experienced far more stress than I due to the frequency with which they were placed in harm's way.

When we did engage with the enemy, it was in very close combat because of the terrain, the trees and rivers, and our tactics. Our company was anywhere between five to three hundred metres from the insurgents. In one instance, Mark Shepherd, my senior platoon commander, dropped grenades on the enemy from the other side of the wall. This proximity and intimacy made our engagements very visceral because we could hear the Taliban changing magazines, breathing, moving. We would hear clicking and know that they had more ammo coming our way.

On April 22, my group was tasked with providing a reaction force in support of a Special Forces mission. I can't really discuss the details, but as a result of some criteria not being met, the mission was aborted and we left the area earlier than planned, around four in the morning.

A couple of vehicles ahead of us went through a choke point and we followed behind. The next thing I knew there was a big fireball and everyone inside our light armoured vehicle (LAV) was rocked. We had hit a mine.

I had been standing up in the crew commander's hatch, my chest, shoulders, and head exposed, when I was thrown back into the turret. I felt an intense heat, and a pressure wave throwing me back and travelling through my body from the bottom up. In the aftermath, my ears were ringing and I felt something like vertigo. My gunner and driver got banged around pretty bad, as did the Special Forces guys in the back, but we were okay.

The protocol was a drill—evasive action—so everybody else got out to do their "fives and twenties," circling around the vehicle at increasing distances, but I was no good. I crawled out of the turret. The radio wasn't completely working, but I could hear Mark communicate with our battalion headquarters and assume my call sign, which meant that I was either dead or out of commission (*hors de combat*). We had just hit a mine, and yet that was one of the most painful moments, because I knew I was a liability for the team. I felt like I had put my men in danger.

I remember thinking I had to make it to my sergeant major, Steven Jeans, in the vehicle behind us, but I couldn't really walk. I kept falling down, so I crawled my way towards him and pulled myself on top of the deck of his vehicle to talk to him. I must have been a babbling idiot; I think we later joked about it with each other.

Meanwhile, the troops did a recovery of the vehicle and discovered that our right forward wheel had hit an anti-tank mine, an AT6 to be precise. Those bad boys were meant for tanks, but we hit it with an LAV. The group managed to chain up the damaged wheel wells, and they drove that LAV with multiple flat wheels an hour back to the patrol base. That's incredible technology. I later met some of the guys at GDLS Canada (manufacturer of the LAV3) and told them how they saved our lives.

Back at the patrol base, I got checked out by the medics. I wasn't bleeding, but I was in a lot of pain, so they medicated me and gave me a sedative to sleep. After that, things started getting weird.

I began experiencing massive acid reflux and sharp chest pains, so bad that I would sleep with my vest on tight so that I wouldn't inhale deeply. If I did, I would get a sharp pain and wake up. I had numbness in my hands too. I had to clip my rifle to my load-bearing vest and carry it with one hand because I kept dropping it. I was an idiot for thinking that my condition wasn't a big deal.

The medical team in the field treated me for anxiety and pain and was very good at keeping me level and competent without making me numb. These people are extremely gifted. They can take someone who has been blown up and help them enough to still do what they need to do. In my case, that was to bring every soldier home.

From April to August, we did countless operations, dismounted, and engaged in combat. We collectively walked over 600 km as a company group. As a result of that experience I was honoured with my Medal of Military Valour, but I didn't do what they said I did for myself. I did it because I was in a company group of four hundred warriors, men and women, and I had an obligation to them. I loved my job and I knew I was good at it. In hindsight, it makes me sad to think that the thing I was best at was taking lives and putting people in harm's way.

As the months went by in theatre, my anxiety grew because I knew from a mathematics perspective that I would soon lose soldiers. There's always a risk, and part of our officer training is based on the force ratio and combat estimates in Staff College and in combat team commander's courses. Every time we went out on a mission, I felt that worry, but death didn't come. The next time, I was even more anxious, and the next, and the next. After a while, I didn't want to go out anymore because it was just a matter of time before we would have a catastrophic event. Miraculously, I didn't lose a single soldier.

But my anxiety changed how I treated my troops. I became much more extreme, much more polarizing. When there was an error, I was very hard on them, but when things were done right, I was overly emotional and thankful. I was a pendulum swinging from one side to the other.

Since my tour, I've spoken to the leadership team that was with me in Afghanistan, and they told me things I hadn't even realized. They watched me, the way I functioned, and they saw me fall apart, but they were loyal. They protected me, not only physically on the battlefield but also emotionally. That's something that's hard to forget.

People think soldiers are harsh, but they act that way to protect themselves, because underneath they're not really that hard. They have soft sides. My worst days in the army were my best days as a human because I felt real unconditional love. These are the stories I'll tell my girls when they get older.

———

When I returned to Canada, I was posted to another headquarters job, then to the Staff College in Toronto (pre-colonel school) to do my master's degree. I used that time to do physio and look after my body. I tried to come off my medication, but it didn't go well. I wasn't able to sleep and my left side was in a lot of pain. But I built my body up strong enough that I could mitigate the discomfort.

After I finished my degree, I was promoted to lieutenant colonel and made the chief of operations for the Canadian Special Operations Regiment, and all the while I tried to hide that my body was failing me. I continued to experience recurring pain in my head behind my neck, and sometimes my leg would give way and I would collapse. I had a number of tests done, and I started seeing a headache specialist and sleep therapist. I was given a variety of neurological drugs, including some antidepressants to change the serotonin levels in my brain, but I hated that because I felt like I was a nanosecond behind my normal thought process. Being impaired without pain was worse than being completely clear and uncomfortable.

The military humbled me yet again with an appointment to command an infantry battalion in 3 RCR, and that was the pinnacle of my career. A top honour for an infantry officer. We don't command anything more purely than that. I was thrilled—I was going to a battalion with paratroopers and all the fun stuff. I foolishly thought I could hide my injuries.

I soon found out that the 2 Canadian Mechanized Brigade Group leadership had to do the Army Iron Man competition, a 50 km race that includes rucksack, canoe portage, and solo paddle. One day, I was training in the unit and I put a canoe on my head and started running, but the canoe yolk pushed on my neck in such a way that I blacked out and collapsed. Of course, once the canoe hit the ground, it popped off my neck and I was fine. I explained what happened to Mike Crouzat, a doctor on the base and friend of mine, and he was puzzled and told me to monitor it. In the meantime, I got the material technicians in the unit to build me a yolk for my rucksack which allowed me to hook the canoe onto my rucksack above my head and not put pressure on my neck. Other than my regimental sergeant major (RSM), Keith Olstad, and my wife, I didn't tell anyone and continued to train as if nothing was wrong.

Looking back I know it was selfish of me not to admit that I had limitations, but my injury wasn't obvious on the outside. I hadn't reached my breaking point.

In 2012, I was at home with my youngest daughter, Willow. She was about six months old at the time. I was holding her in my left hand, making the bed, when my hand and arm gave out and collapsed. Willow dropped onto the bed below her and giggled, but I was stunned. What had just happened?

This came about a week before my battalion was scheduled to do a major joint airmobile exercise with the 82nd Airborne at Fort Bragg, North Carolina. This opportunity was a big deal for me and my team, and I couldn't just put it off. So I left and tried to put my physical ailments out of mind.

Soon enough I was jumping out of a C-17 with my battalion, and as I exited the aircraft, I saw about fifteen hundred other jumpers in the air around me. I remember thinking, *Holy cow, this is a cool life. It's a visual masterpiece.* Just then, my left side went entirely limp. Luckily, the single-point release system for the American parachute was close to my right side and I was able to pull it to release my equipment before I hit the ground. Once I landed, I thought, *Okay, apparently I'm pretty injured. I need to fix this today.* I told the RSM that something was not right, and we powered through our four-day exercise and focused on getting back to Petawawa.

Back in Canada, Mike and I got much more aggressive and did a series of MRIs that revealed I had scarring on the left side of my brain and neurological and C-spine damage from my accident four years earlier. The neurological system is like a tree, and our limbs, like the branches. The blast was like a tornado, and when it went through my body, it knocked down some branches and leaves, but my neurological system still looked like a tree. It still functioned, but it didn't have the same structure.

I remember when Mike gave me the medical chit, the Medical Employment Limitations, outlining my injuries. It meant I had breached the Canadian Forces Universality of Service Clause, and therefore had to leave the Canadian Forces. I was very familiar with the process as I had exited many injured soldiers as the battalion commander, but it was a huge blow to take personally.

I took the chit over to Simon Hetherington, my brigade commander and a good friend, and I sat down in his office and just started weeping.

"I'm broken. This is the end of my career," I told him.

Without a second thought, Simon asked, "Dave, you are going to be okay, what can I do?" He was concerned about me, my family, and my dignity.

We talked and I told him I needed to go home, which I did. I had a bit of a cry, then called my wife, who came home to comfort me.

To add insult to injury, the next month HRH Prince Philip, the Colonel and Chief of the RCR, was scheduled to arrive in Toronto to oversee the consecration of 3 RCR's regimental colours. The previous colours were damaged and therefore needed to be replaced. We had been planning the HRH visit for an entire year. Mike didn't want me doing the parade, but I was still the commanding officer of the battalion, and I was stubborn and too proud to step aside. The battalion performed incredibly, and we demonstrated a truly beautiful display of discipline and regimental history. I was so honoured to be a part of that ceremony, and it allowed me the dignity to say I walked away doing the best I could.

My two-year command appointment was drawing to a close. On June 6, 2013, I gave up command of 3 RCR on the banks of the Ottawa River in an unorthodox change-of-command parade that showcased the operational capability of my entire battalion team in a "field" environment. The soldiers, command leadership team, and I parachuted into the river, amphibious landed, and swam to the shores of the beach. This was my last day standing in uniform as a real soldier, and it was the hardest speech I had ever had to give. I said goodbye to the unit and thanked the chain of command, my family and friends. I was so proud, and felt strong and included, but at the same time I also felt fragile, scared, and alone. I was saying goodbye to the only thing I had ever known.

After serving in all three of our battalions, I got to end my career in one, and that was very bittersweet. I gave the military my whole life, everything I had. I loved it.

It feels like a lifetime since I transitioned into my new life. Some things will never go away or leave my mind. I know I see the world through a different set of lenses, and that is what makes me who I am today. Wars are started because of hatred but fought by those that never stop loving. I would go anywhere on the planet with my troops in 2 RCR because they did just that. All my time in the regiment taught me not only about who I was but, most important, who I wanted to be; I wanted to be just like the soldiers. The stories from veterans of WWII and Korea I heard as a young subaltern never mentioned the dog-shit battle stuff. The veterans talked about the people who were alongside them. The reason they were so great had nothing to do with the tactics, but everything to do with the soldier from Corner Brook, Newfoundland, or Markham, Ontario, that just happened to say, "I'm here because I love you and I will make sure you do not fail." And I think sharing stories of camaraderie and trust is more important today than ever before. *Pro Patria* (For Country).

Lieutenant Colonel David Quick (Ret), SMV, CD, MBA, joined the army in 1994 and went on to serve for twenty years with all three battalions of the Royal Canadian Regiment. During his career he was deployed to Bosnia, Kosovo, Haiti, and Afghanistan, where he received the Star of Military Valour for his actions. In 2014, he was recruited by the True Patriot Love Foundation to co-lead the largest expedition of its kind, a trip that paired injured military veterans and prominent Canadian business leaders to trek unsupported to the North Pole. David has two daughters, lives in downtown Toronto, and works in the finance industry.

In the Zhari district on Operation Dragon Strike, one of our many planned operations.

Marching proudly with Prince Phillip and 3 RCR during the consecration of the regiment's colours. I'm on the right.

THREE BROTHERS IN ARMS

A Call to Arms

CORPORAL D. BRETT IRWIN (RET)

*Bullets were snapping all around, landing on my feet.
It was like a stereotypical movie battle scene, only it
was happening to me, and it was a lot scarier.*

The day I was leaving for Afghanistan, my family came to Petawawa to see me off. My dad and mom, stepmom and stepdad, sister and grandmother—the whole family. All the soldiers who were shipping out were surrounded by their families. But there wasn't a bus in sight. They put us all into formation and said, "We're not leaving today." Turns out there was a volcano erupting in Iceland, covering half of Europe with smoke and ash, so all flights were grounded. Instead of heading off to battle, we were going on a forty-eight–hour stand-down.

I went back home to Brampton to hang out with family and friends. Two days later, the volcano was still spewing ash. I figured we wouldn't be going anywhere, but I had to report for duty anyway. My mom hopped into the car with me, and we drove back to Petawawa together, arriving right on time at 6:30 in the morning. As we drove around the corner into the base, both of us spotted the buses at the same time. There were about fifteen, all lined up and waiting. My mom broke down. I could tell she was trying to hold it together but couldn't. By the time I had to climb onto my assigned bus, she was sobbing. I hugged her. I couldn't help but think that this might be the last time I ever get to hug her, so I made it a really tight one. All I could see as we drove off was her standing there, in the same spot, crying.

I had wanted to be in the army ever since I was in the fourth grade playing cops and robbers. I remember I was a cop chasing bad guys and I thought, *This is awesome. I want to chase bad guys for a living.* I was just a kid then, but years later, when I heard that Canadians were going to Afghanistan to fight with the Americans after 9/11, I knew I had to join the military and fight for my country. It was a call to arms. I had to join to be true to myself. That's how I found myself saying goodbye to my mother in April of 2010.

We slept in holes we'd dug the first couple of days in our new camp—Combat Outpost Panjshir—in Afghanistan. It was an incredibly austere position out in the field. We brought in a tank with a big scoop on the front to create berms to surround us, which we slept behind until we built the area into a functional camp. But we were always building it. We would go on a morning patrol, come back, and shovel dirt and fill sandbags, then go out on a night patrol. I remember thinking that if I never had to fill another sandbag, I'd be happy. Factor in the constant security we were doing at the camp, and we were going on maybe thirty minutes of sleep a day. Being uncomfortable became normal.

In May, things began to heat up. Mike LeClair, our section commander, was a real go-getter. He wanted to bring the fight to the enemy, so when we got into a big firefight on May 25, we hit back hard. I was in the rear of the pack. We'd been in contact before with IEDs, but never in a gunfight. At first, I didn't even know what was happening. I heard bullets being fired, but didn't know we were being shot at because I'd never had anything fired directly at me. I just saw everyone run and take cover against the wall and start returning fire. I stood there in the open on the road, then thought, *Oh, I better take cover.* I started shooting but didn't know what I was shooting at; I was just really excited to be in a gunfight, shooting a gun. I was like, "Holy shit, we're in a gunfight."

When you're an infantry soldier, you spend such a long time doing nothing but training and preparing yourself to simply get to do your job. So the moment I realized that I was actually getting to do my job was extremely cool. The guys in the front who had bullets snapping around them probably thought differently, but, for me, seeing everything coming together the way it did from the back was wild. We just started shooting in the general direction of where the enemy was. Honestly, it was awesome.

The next day, we left camp sometime around zero dark stupid in the morning to patrol around a little town called Little Chalghowr. I was the point guy for the Canadians. We hit an open field with a large wall on one side and another short wall about a metre high and two hundred metres long that divided the field in half. While I was skirting the tall wall, a couple of Afghan National Army guys in front of me were able to set up in fighting position along the short wall. There was a bit of a language barrier, so I asked my section to communicate with them over the radio to find out what was going on.

While I waited, I decided to take a short halt and sat down on a little hump. I'd just gotten my back against the high wall, when a burst of machine gun fire came in only a couple of inches from me. The Taliban had opened fire on us. Dirt from the wall bounced off and hit my face. I fell to the ground. I looked back up to where I'd been sitting, and the whole area was imploding. It was terrifying. I couldn't crawl forward, I couldn't crawl backwards. I was frozen stiff. The volley only went on for about twenty seconds, but it felt like an eternity.

My whole section was shooting back as best they could, but they were trying to move up in position at the same time. I looked to my right and saw them standing in an extended line abreast with my position, and as soon as I saw that, I thought, *This is it.* I jumped and madly dashed for twenty metres or so to get to that short wall where the Afghan Army guys were set up. There was another barrage coming in from the Taliban, but I made it, and we all took up fighting positions with them. We exchanged fire for a couple of minutes, then an order from Mike came in: four of us were to go over the wall and storm the Taliban position. I thought, *Dude, you're absolutely crazy.* There was still a lot of fire, the position was about two hundred metres away, and there was absolutely no cover. But it was the army, and we didn't have a choice.

On the count of three, everyone started providing covering fire, and over the wall I went. I started running, then looked back. I was maybe ten metres down, not even. Maybe ten feet. That's when everyone else started hopping over the wall. I kind of stuttered for a second and stopped—I wanted them to catch up to me. Bullets were snapping all around, landing on my feet. It was like a stereotypical movie battle scene, only it was happening to me, and it was a lot scarier. We sprinted, and as we got closer to the enemy, they stopped shooting and took off. When we finally made it across the field, I felt as though I'd run a marathon—adrenaline was pumping through my body, but I felt incredibly tired. Mike's orders were right. Without any casualties, we took the enemy position and captured one of their vehicles and a motorcycle.

After that, we encountered the Taliban almost every day.

———

On June 4, 2010, we went on a patrol and knew we were going to get into a fight. After being in so many fights, we'd start placing bets on the map of where we'd end up getting ambushed by the Taliban. I got pretty good at guessing—I'd get it down to within a hundred metres.

It was hot that day. Super, super hot. At the time I weighed in at 145 pounds, but I'd go out at just shy of 300—I had to carry grenades, twelve hundred bullets, even a rocket launcher. I was fully loaded for battle because we never knew when we were going to get into one. Mike gave the order for the section to split in two. The back half of the section swept out and set up a fire base; we were going to act as bait to get contact so they could level the Taliban. I was point man again. Justin, a good friend of mine, Mike, and I continued over a wall, then stopped; we could hear the Taliban. They weren't yelling, just talking at a normal volume. I couldn't believe it. We were in the middle of a grape field, and they were right there with us. We had two options: go for the high ground and a gunfight, or sweep around and take the lower ground, but I was pretty positive there'd be a bomb there. We took the high ground. Eventually two other guys were able to reach us. We started pushing.

The Taliban were thirty metres away. It was the closest contact I'd had. They stood up on the other side of the wall and opened fire. They were directly in front of us, shooting right at us, all across our front-age. I can't tell you how many of them there were, but it felt like there were a hundred bullets blazing by every second. I have no words to describe how loud it was, how unbelievable that sound is when all that fire is exploding around you. I stumbled forward and jumped—it was a six-foot drop because the grape fields there are so tall, so I bunkered in hard. Justin jumped into the same row as me, and as he landed, his rocket launcher punched me right in the face. I thought he knocked my teeth out. I scrambled to my feet and lifted my machine gun over my head—I couldn't see anything over the grapevines—then jumped and unloaded the full belt in the direction of the enemy. Beneath the roar of the gunfire, I heard a weird sound and knew it was Mike. A minute later, I could hear him on the radio.

"One, this is one alpha. I'm hit, I'm hit, I'm hit."

I thought, *Holy shit, now we're in it.* All of a sudden, rocket-propelled grenades were screaming over our heads. I blasted my C-9 LMG (light machine gun) again. It jammed; I threw it down, grabbed my rocket launcher off my backpack, and climbed back to the top of the row. Bullets were spitting past us from all sides. I had to shoot the rocket, but I'd only ever shot one once before, in training. When you're in shit like that, it's hard to think, which is why we train so repetitively—we need that muscle memory. But I forgot how to do it. I had to look at the side of the rocket, at the instructions written there. I know that sounds ridiculous: that I had to stop in the middle of a gunfight to take the time to read instructions, but I had to shoot the rocket. And I did it. The thing arced off at a forty-five-degree angle right into the air. Literally the worst shot you've ever seen with a rocket launcher.

Mike called my burst in, then yelled to Justin, "Come here!" There was so much fire coming directly at us, we couldn't help but think that Justin's exposing himself like that would be suicide. But Mike said it again. I looked at Justin.

"Cover me," he said.

I cleared the stoppage in my C-9 and started blasting, and Justin crawled up the embankment behind me. I couldn't even look where I was shooting; I just kept my eyes on Justin. He was slipping and sliding in the dirt—it's not like it's super-easy to climb when you're wearing all that gear—and I could see bullets landing, somehow hitting between his knees and arms. He was crawling, and they were flying right underneath his belly. I thought, I'm about to see one of my really good friends get killed here, but I just kept blasting until he was able to get up and run across the maybe eight or ten feet to where our section commander was.

I found out later that Mike had been shot in the arm, and his side was all ripped up. He needed Justin to do first aid. He'd been shot in the chest too, but his plate saved his life; it just shredded the magazines he was wearing around his chest. Because he was injured, I had to take a leadership position. I became third in command. We got the patrol consolidated and the commander in a helicopter, then got out of there ourselves. When we cut the gear off Mike and did an inventory on his stuff, we saw something that looked like body fat until I realized it was just the apple pack from his rations.

The rest of the summer, no matter where we were in Afghanistan, it started to feel as though the Taliban were always shooting at us. Peter McKay, minister of national defence, and General Walter Natynczyk even came to visit in Chinook helicopters to give us all a pat on the back for all the fighting we'd done. The day they left, the Taliban started shooting at our camp.

We didn't always return fire. It got to the point where they'd be shooting, and we'd be sitting around watching DVDs on our personal laptops, hear the bullets echoing away, lean out to make sure no one had gotten hurt, then just go back to watching our DVDs. We got completely desensitized to being shot at. It sounds bizarre, but it became the norm when a gunfight was happening every day. The days when it didn't happen, we'd wonder what was going on. Did we just kill a bunch of them the day before? Don't they have the fight to bring it to us? Then the next day, they'd start shooting at us again. Maybe they had just had someone's birthday the day before and went out partying. Who knew?

———

When you leave for deployment, you don't know when you're coming back until about thirty days before. I knew I had put my mother through hell when I left, so when my trip home was set in stone, I decided to surprise her. I told her that even though the rest of my group was coming home, I was going to stick back for another month. I wouldn't be in danger, I told her. I'd be in Kandahar Airfield, making a little bit of extra money helping pack everything up. She believed me. Of course, she cursed me for everything I was and told me to come home immediately.

We had four days in Cyprus doing our decompression, which also involved a lot of partying, so I had to make sure I stayed out of any pictures. We flew home, had two days in Petawawa, then cleared out for home. It was a Wednesday, my mom's bowling night. So I got into my fatigues and my combat boots, and my buddy drove me to where she bowls. At eight o'clock in the evening, I walked in in full uniform, thinking my mom would be easy to spot, but there were almost forty bowling lanes. I thought, *Oh my gosh, she's going to see me before I see her.* Luckily, someone in her league recognized me and showed me where she was.

She had just finished a frame, so I rushed over, and as soon as she turned around she saw me. She looked like she lost her mind; her hands shook in front of her mouth. It was an amazing moment to see how happy and excited she was to see me, to see her realize that I was officially home and out of danger. Then over the PA system, someone said, "Wendy's son just got off the plane from Afghanistan and is here to surprise his mother." The whole alley erupted in cheers and clapping. I was crying and she was crying.

I found out later that I actually boarded the plane to leave Kandahar at almost the same moment my sister was giving birth to my nephew Logan. Every time I tell people that story, they just say, "Cool, now tell me more gunfight stories." My life was never the same from the moment I left for Afghanistan to the moment I came home—it was changed forever. That gunfire skipping off that wall—I can still feel the sensation of the dirt hitting me in the face. That was the closest call I ever had. I'll never forget it. But Logan being born at the same time that I leave?! That's crazy! It's like two new lives beginning at the same time.

Corporal D. Brett Irwin (Ret) joined the Queen's York Rangers in 2005 and served for two years before joining 3 RCR Oscar Company. He lives with his fiancée in Angus, Ontario.

With my grandma and her husband, George, in Petawawa, just a few days before I was supposed to deploy.

Taken after our very first gunfight in May. We're still covered in sweat and just looking forward to getting some real food to eat, not rations. I'm second from the right.

Here we are holding our regimental flag at COP Panjshir. I'm wearing the baseball cap.

I took this photo of my C-6 GPM (general purpose machine gun) at OP Nightmare, a local compound that we took over. In the distance is a broken tree where one of our men lost a leg, and close by is a place we dubbed "Sketchy Mosque" because it was known for insurgent activity.

Bravery Under Fire

CORPORAL JUSTIN BRONZAN

A month in, and temperatures were soaring above forty-five degrees Celsius by midday, and as the mercury rose, so did the fighting.

I was nineteen when I joined the army. Even as a kid, I had always looked up to those who served in the military. Of course, I loved the movies and the video games, but really I was fascinated by WWII and big operations like D-Day. Like my heroes, I felt a similar sense of duty to my country. When things in Afghanistan started to heat up, I was in college taking engineering, but my heart wasn't in it. I saw the chance to be a part of what Canadians were doing in the Middle East, and I left school and signed up. I did my training and got assigned to the 3 RCR, but going to Afghanistan was on my bucket list. Finally, two years later, I was told I was being deployed. I was thrilled.

We arrived in Kandahar on April 19, 2010, and to my disappointment, there wasn't a lot going on. The guys we relieved even said that their tour had been pretty boring. Summer in Afghanistan was just beginning and it was very hot and very dusty.

For the first month, we stayed at a dilapidated school, but the higher-ups wanted us at an outpost about a half mile north, in a vast field of short mud-walled opium plantations. Patches of eight-foot-tall cannabis plants scattered the canvas of the south Panjwai plain around our new base on Route Nightmare: COP Panjshir.

Of course, there was no building out there, so during those first few weeks, we started building a compound. Aside from one armoured bulldozer, the construction was all done by hand. Throughout our whole tour we were consistently building it. We'd go out on patrols during the day, come home to base, and continue working. It was our own little world.

———

Early on, before we had seen any action, we were rotated in shifts on a small observation post where every few minutes a car or a motorcycle would go by. There were so many motorcycles in Afghanistan, and no one would believe how much they fit on one bike: Dad, Mom, three kids, and seven bags. It was impressive. We had been out there for hours and were starting to get bored, so we figured we should do something. We decided that, every couple of vehicles, we were going to stop one, talk to them, and have a look at the vehicle.

Soon enough we saw a guy on a motorcycle barrelling towards us. We stopped him and asked him to get off his bike and did the whole drill. I noticed he had a few saddlebags on the bike, so I opened one. Inside were all these wires and batteries. I thought, *Who is this guy?* He could be setting up speakers or making bombs. When we searched him, we found a ton of money.

With the help of our interpreter we discovered that he was the town's mullah, their religious leader. Of course, we didn't know this before we stopped and searched him, but the people in the town were obviously not happy with us and formed a small protest near our outpost. I was with Brett and my buddies Jared and Steven, and we said to one another, "We're going to die tonight." We thought if there was ever a time that they would do anything, it would be when we were sitting in the middle of the dark at this outpost. We were ready, but nervous. I remember we mentally prepared what we would do, how we'd place different things and set up our sandbags.

But nothing happened! Later on, we realized what real encounters were like, and by then, this seemed like just a training episode, something that taught us to be on our toes when we needed to be.

Shortly after we moved from the school to COP Panjshir, Mike LeClair, our section commander, came into our tent and told us we were going on a night patrol to a suspected IED factory. We stood around the table, the map came out, and we did our thing.

I was not a fan of night patrols, but orders were orders, so we stepped off in the order of march and headed out. Closer to the town, we came to a short grassy field, probably waist height. That's not exactly short grass by our standards, but for there, it was. We pushed on through the field, but it was dark. Dark, dark, dark. We had night-vision goggles, so the darkness wasn't as overwhelming.

We saw a little hut in front of us, but noticed something moving in front. There was a bull, a massive bull, chained to a post. And he could smell us. I got my gun ready and thought, *Sorry, bull, but between me or you, you're going to get it.* The bull started to freak out, and even though it was a good-sized chain, he was so strong, he snapped it. I thought he was going to charge at us, but luckily, he took off in another direction.

We waited a minute, then Mike split us up to check the hut out.

He went with Steve and another guy towards the hut and found two guys sleeping. How they didn't hear the bull, I don't know, but Mike shined flashlights in their eyes and they woke up fast. We looked in the hut, but there weren't any bomb parts or explosives inside, just opium drying.

I thought the whole thing was sketchy, but Mike signalled for us to keep going, so we stepped off once more and continued our patrol into the town. There was no traffic, no lights, nothing. We passed by a mosque that we had nicknamed "Sketchy Mosque"—we knew it was connected to the insurgents—but everything was quiet. Unnervingly quiet. The moon shone bright, but all the buildings were made of layers of mud (then packed with more mud), so there was no moonlight reflected anywhere. We continued on in complete silence until the sound of barking exploded above us. On the rooftops all around us were big Afghani dogs watching us.

Apart from the shock of the dogs, nothing happened, but I was spooked, and I'm sure others were too. Of course, no one would admit it.

All in all, it was pretty quiet for the first month we were there. We did a lot of presence patrols—walking around, making our presence known, and checking out the area—but we were also able to build relationships with the Afghan people, especially the kids. They'd come to the outposts we occupied and we'd give them pens, candy, and the rations we didn't want to eat. In the school, we held a bunch of shirras, which were like council meetings with the elders of the area, our interpreters, and our platoon commander. These meetings were all about balance. We had to make sure that we protected all parties.

But soon enough, we would see action.

A month in, and temperatures were soaring above forty-five degrees Celsius by midday, and as the mercury rose, so did the fighting.

My first firefight was May 25. We were conducting a presence patrol, walking through opium fields, when we came up over a typical short wall that fenced in the grape fields. We went over the little wall and had proceeded into the grape field when all of a sudden I heard a *snap snap snap*. Bullets were coming in overhead! Mike, our section commander, quickly had the front group form a fire base so they could engage the Taliban on a front. Then he called me and my buddies Brett, Jared, and Steve and told us what he wanted us to do: charge across the two-hundred-yard stretch to get behind the Taliban position and flank them. As soon as he said, "You've got to go, you've got to go," I thought, *I guess I'm running across this field now. I really hope I don't get shot.*

In full kit, we charged across the grape field as the rest of our section gave covering fire. I remember bullets singing overtop of us. Fortunately, at the time, engagements with the Taliban were so slow that they usually retreated after a couple of minutes. Our first encounter with the Taliban was over almost as soon as it began. For the next two months, we would see more and more of those engagements, and they would escalate.

We were constantly covered in dust and grime. By June, I had maybe showered twice since being off the plane, because we didn't have working showers at the outpost. Whenever we did a supply run back to the main base, we got to use their facilities, but we had to be quick and mind the "Three Minutes" sign.

On June 4, I was sitting on my dusty cot when I heard the warning order for another presence patrol. No problem, we'd done those before.

It must have been nearly 4 p.m. when we set off rank and file—or, as we say, in the order of march—because although it was hot (when wasn't it?), you could tell the sun had peaked, which meant we might have a respectable amount of shade. We took a different path than normal because Mike wanted to mix it up and keep the Taliban guessing. As we continued down the double-wide gravel road, we looked for those signs. IEDs. Like many in my battle group, I was good at finding them, and given our new route, it was important to keep our eyes peeled.

We were constantly on the lookout for IEDs. We'd go on patrol and find one, then wait for the explosive guys to come and do their thing. Every day was the same. There'd be a fight, then we'd find an IED, or we'd find an IED, then there would be a fight. Sometimes, we would be double on patrol, so we'd end up getting to fight in the morning, then finding an IED later. It was like a constant Whac-A-Mole treasure hunt.

We walked through the cannabis and grape fields, lying low, then stopped for a short halt and had some water and smokes. And snuck a few grapes—they were incredible there.

Brett was saying something, but I thought I heard voices, so I said, "Shut up. Shh!"

Faintly, we could hear talking, and it was getting closer.

We signalled for Mike, and he moved up to the concealed row of grapes to meet us with his typical "What's up, boys?" He was the kind of commander who would tell you anything straight up. We respected but also feared him, as it should be with any good sergeant.

When we explained what we heard, he asked if we were sure, then quickly decided to split off a small detachment from our patrol to satellite our position. As we re-formed the main body, we began handrailing the grape field: we walked parallel with the gravel road, and the satellite unit crossed and j-hooked around a small drying hut to set up a flank if necessary.

As we (the main body) continued on, I began to feel as if I had reached a brief moment of anxious clarity. Brett was directly in front of me at that point, and I said to him, "Dude, I got the fuckin' heebie jeebies."

"What?" he said.

I repeated myself, and he answered, "Hey bro, we're good, man."

Then everything erupted.

The *rat tat tattling* of multiple AK-47s and RPKs ripped in my ears as I scrambled forward to look for cover. I felt like I was moving in slow motion. Blindly, I dove headfirst six feet into the grape field row below, landing on top of Brett, and, it turned out, slamming his face with my gun. As we stood up, we both uttered a *holy shit*. The rows were taller than we were and our patrol, satellite detachment, and enemy fire blazed overtop of us. We were trapped in the middle.

We started shooting, then Brett yelled through the noise, "DO YOU HEAR THAT?"

A voice was coming from the row behind us. It was Mike. "Bronzan! I'm hit. Get over here!"

Brett and I thought for a second and looked at each other.

I shouted back, "Sarge, they're shooting on all sides. I can't!"

Then I heard, "GET THE FUCK OVER HERE!" And I knew I had to; he was my fire-team partner. It was not an order, or a choice. It's what we do.

"Brett, I need covering fire."

"Dude, the dirt mound is taller than me," he replied, but he lifted up his 5.56mm belt-fed whippersnapper over his head and began to unload sporadically towards the enemy, and I scrambled over the mound. It felt like bumblebees were zipping past me as I jumped blindly to the other side.

"I'm shot, Bronzan," Mike said calmly. I noticed a bullet hole through his right forearm and had begun to assess it when Mike pointed to his left side and said, "No, here, look."

I moved his left arm and saw that his vest was soaked with blood. I opened his TAC vest and frag and tore his shirt, but blood began spurting out of his chest.

Luckily for Mike, the bullet didn't go through his chest, but tracked his outer rib cage and came out his back skin. He was in a lot of pain and had lost a shitload of blood, but I knew his organs were good. He started to get clammy and pale, but I told him he would be okay and applied pressure until the medic could arrive. A complete circus roared on overhead. Then, *boom!*

One of our guys had launched a M72 rocket. The intense reverberation rattled my bones, and immediate nausea from the concussion set in. In retaliation to the Taliban's RPGs, our weapons detachment sent two 84mm recoilless rounds, also known as "the show stopper," screaming overhead. Finally, after thirty minutes, the mayhem calmed as the remaining Taliban retreated.

Within minutes, Lindsay, our high-spirited medic, slid down the edge of the grape mound in the dry crumbled mud and started assessing and asking questions. I told her what I thought, and she called on Troy, who was one of our patrol casualty-care specialists, to assist her with the casualty. I took Troy's machine gun in exchange for my rifle, and set out for a hole in the cordon that the remainder of the patrol had formed. As I walked, the adrenaline surging through me began to taper off, but my heart was still pounding. Then I saw a man pulling a wheelbarrow of hay with his son. They stopped and looked at me, and I knew the firefight was officially over. To them it was just an average day; to me it was some crazy story.

After a while, a medivac helicopter hovered over the grape field and lowered a casualty basket. Mike got loaded, and off went the bird.

The sun began to shoulder the horizon as dusk arrived. Charlie section met us on the exfil (exfiltration) to give us their LAVs so we could get back to camp. They walked back themselves.

It was quiet in the LAV. One of our sergeants poked his head around and said, "Boys, I know it sucks, but we will go out again." Everyone looked around at one another, but we already knew we'd be going back. We wanted our revenge.

After that, we fought every morning and afternoon. The Taliban were back, and they fought like hell.

————————

During my tour, I had the opportunity to develop a very close relationship with our interpreter, Omar. We had other interpreters come in, but Omar was the only one with us from start to finish, and he was well respected. As we patrolled more and had more encounters with the Taliban, I thought that Omar should be armed, to protect himself, and it bothered me that we couldn't give him weapons because he was technically a noncombatant.

On more than one occasion, I'd say to him, "Omar, you're crazy for being out here, you realize this?"

And he'd say to me, "Well, why, Mr. Bronzan?"

"You're out here with no weapons and it's the middle of a fight!"

He'd answer with his usual nonchalance. "Mr. Bronzan, I live here my whole life with no weapons and I'm still alive."

He always made me laugh with that.

Because I was the section commander's fire-team partner and scribe, Omar and I worked together a lot and would often be close in the order of march. Patrols last a lot longer than anybody probably realizes, and for half the patrol we were generally sitting down listening and looking. So Omar and I had many conversations, and I learned about his culture and his religion, and we traded insights on how we thought things were or should be.

I have the utmost admiration for Omar. He's my age, but he's had a hard life. His parents died when he was ten or twelve because of the war, and as our interpreter, he put his life in constant risk. From an Afghan perspective, he was technically acting in the interest of an invasive force. We got to pack up and go home at the end of our tour, but he had to stay and live there.

We left in November, and I lost contact with Omar for about four or five months, until I finally found him on Facebook, and then we kept in touch regularly through Facebook and email.

In 2013, ISAF left Afghanistan altogether, so the Taliban and the Afghan forces were fighting constantly. Things got pretty bad for Omar. The Taliban began contracting out killings of anyone who had acted as an interpreter for ISAF. I'm not sure if they ever identified him, but his situation got so bad that we both agreed that he should leave. The Taliban were like the mafia; they were coming, whether we liked it or not. Omar sold everything that he and his family didn't absolutely need, to get the funds to leave. Then he travelled through Iran to Turkey where he attempted to make it to Greece on one of those half-inflated rubber dinghies with plywood in them.

The boat capsized. He woke up in the hospital a couple of days later, and the doctor said he should have died with the amount of sea water he had swallowed. But he was desperate and tried again. On this second attempt across the Aegean Sea, he did make it. Now he's in Germany in a refugee camp, and the government is letting him go to university for language studies, but his family is still in Afghanistan, and at this time there is no projected date for their immigration. They are getting by, but we hope that someday they can all come to Canada and our families can meet. Omar and I both have two daughters around the same ages.

I wanted to join the military to be a part of something great. Having done a tour, I have to say that out of everything that happened over there, meeting and befriending Omar was the most memorable and most valuable to me.

Corporal Justin Bronzan joined the Canadian Armed Forces in 2007 and went to Afghanistan in 2010, where he served as a section scribe, LAV gunner, and the section commander's fire team partner. He was awarded a Command Commendation for his actions under fire in Afghanistan. Justin has a keen interest in chemistry, engineering, physics, and cosmology and is currently stationed at CFB Trenton as an aviation systems technician. He lives with his wife and two daughters in Trenton, Ontario.

We learned early on in the construction phase of COP Panjshir to cover our faces during the daily sandstorms. We'd see them coming and cover up so we wouldn't breathe in the sand or get it stuck in our teeth.

I dislocated my shoulder in June. Here I am at COP Panjshir, sitting with Brett, resting up and having some snacks.

We were coming back from visiting a town northwest of our outpost where we found a couple of IEDs. At my feet is a medium rocket; we always took a bunch of these on our patrols.

Soldiering On

Master Corporal Mark Hoogendoorn

There were three trees along a wadi, and they had white flags hanging in them, which we knew meant there were explosives in the area, but it was our job to find them. Over the radio, we heard that the Taliban were watching our every move. Things could get a little bit hairy at any moment.

I grew up in St. Catharines, just outside of Niagara Falls. My grandfather and my great-uncle both served in the Canadian Armed Forces. My grandfather taught my three brothers and me how to shoot, how to live off the land, and how to use maps and compasses out in the wild. It's no surprise all four of us ended up in either the military or emergency services.

I joined the army in 2007 as a combat engineer. I had done a few different jobs and lived on my own, but being a part of the Canadian Forces was always something I wanted to do.

After I finished my training, I was posted to 2 Combat Engineer Regiment in Petawawa and did a tactical combat casualty care (TCCC) course to become a first responder overseas, so that if anyone got injured out on patrol, I could provide medical aid. I also did some high-readiness training the U.S., and in April 2010 I left for Afghanistan. Everyone was fighting for spots to go overseas, including me. Deploying was one of the reasons I'd signed up.

We landed in Kandahar in April, at the beginning of the fighting season. It was essentially the end of the farming season and people were out in their poppy fields and grape fields harvesting. We had a couple of days of briefings, then we were choppered out in a Chinook to FOB Ma'sum Ghar. For a month or so we stayed in a school in a little town in the Panjwai district that the Taliban had once occupied, and we headed out on missions from there. We then built a small COP for our troops out of dirt berms, sandbags, and tarps in a farmer's field. COP Panjshir was right off our locally named road "Route Nightmare." From our austere position, we patrolled regularly through the small town of Little Chalghowr, down the friendly routes of Nightmare, Hellhound, Succubus, and other well-named roads. One day the firefights started, and every day from then on we had contact with the insurgents, whether on patrol or at our compound. That's how it was until the day I left.

As a combat engineer on tour, I was tasked with searching for and uncovering IEDs. On a typical patrol, we would send out three combat engineers. We would generally be third or fourth in the order of march, close to the head of the patrol so that if the infantry or anyone else saw something suspicious they could just shout for us. We'd move up, check for IEDs or mines, and clear the area. We were the ones charged with clearing compounds and searching for weapons caches.

I found my first IED just days into the tour, before we even left the school for COP Panjshir. We were called early in the morning because somebody had been seen digging in the side of the road. We checked, but it turned out it was only a farmer clearing dirt from the irrigation system for his grape fields. By the time we returned to the compound, it was maybe four-thirty or five in the morning and it was just getting light outside. I took off all my kit and I went to go to our "washroom"—we had tubes punched through the walls to the outside. On my way back, I saw some wires sticking out of the ground right in the middle of the compound. Obviously that was strange, so I started excavating, clearing off the ground, and found an IED buried right there. The only reason it hadn't detonated was that one of the wires taped to the battery had come off.

I already knew IEDs could be anywhere, but I did not expect to see one in the compound. After that, we took the time to re-clear absolutely everything. That was the only one there.

On the morning of July 31, I woke up at 2:30 a.m. and made my favourite individual meal pack of wieners and beans and some instant coffee. By sunrise, we were ready to go do a clearance op. The locals had told us that there were IEDs in a particular area where we had been shot at on previous patrols, one just a couple of days ago. We planned to go and talk to the people there and have a look around.

We arrived on-site and spent an hour talking with the locals. They pointed to a field and said that there were IEDs there, but they couldn't show us themselves because the Taliban were watching. They didn't want to risk reprisal from the insurgents.

I never liked standing around doing nothing, so I asked to lead the search. I moved to the front and began clearing the path towards the field. There were three trees along a wadi, and they had white flags hanging in them, which we knew meant there were explosives in the area, but it was our job to find them. I cleared up to one of the trees, and a couple of the guys cleared up to another one. Over the radio, we heard that the Taliban were watching our every move. Things could get a little bit hairy at any moment.

I moved to clear up to the middle tree. My metal detector didn't pick up on anything, but underneath me was a wooden pressure plate covering plastic explosives. I took another step, and the next thing I knew I was lying in the blast seat. I hadn't heard a boom, but my ears were ringing. I thought, *What the fuck just happened?*

Instantly, I felt sick to my stomach. I couldn't hear anything, and I couldn't see anything because all the dust and dirt was blanketing the air around me. I heard gunshots and automatically looked for my rifle. It was lying beside me in the hole, but when I tried to pick it up, I saw it was broken from the blast itself. That's when I looked down and saw my leg had snapped in half at my knee and my foot had come up and hit me under my right armpit. I could see that most of my foot was missing. I was one of the TCCCs out on patrol, so I had my leg bag with me with all my medical stuff in it. My tourniquet was sitting right on my TAC vest, just under a clip, but for the life of me I couldn't get my fingers to undo that clip and get my tourniquet.

As soon as the blast went off, Sergeant Jeff Veinot, my section commander at the time, shouted out to everybody to sound off.

I was the only one who didn't respond, and no one could see me because I was down in a hole under a cloud of dust. I don't remember this happening, but Jeff told me later that he shouted to me, and apparently, all of a sudden, I gave him a thumbs-up, right out of the hole, and yelled, "Somebody come help me. I just blew my leg off."

I do remember thinking that I needed to stop the bleeding, but I still couldn't get to my tourniquet. I thought, *Holy fuck, I'm going to die.* So I grabbed ahold of my left leg at the thigh and just squeezed as hard as I could to try and stop the bleeding.

Meanwhile we had a blocking party just south of us taking all the fire. Bullets were flying everywhere. A couple of my engineer buddies, Sean Stinson and Trevor Hamer, cleared up to me very cautiously because often there was a second IED in the area and we didn't want any more casualties. Once they got to me, they grabbed my TAC vest and hauled me out of the hole. Sean put the tourniquet on me and started bandaging me up along with Rick Cicero and Thys Kleyn, a couple of dog handlers we had. Rick had just joined us a couple of weeks earlier, but Thys had been there long before us.

My body had gone into shock. I was hearing booms all around me and kept asking, "Did you guys check for secondaries? Did someone else just get hurt?"

I remember them reassuring me, "It's RPGs, don't worry about it." The ANA was with us and they were trading off fire with the insurgents.

The boys patched me up, tried to bandage my foot as best they could, to keep it clean. By the time the medic arrived maybe twenty minutes later, my leg had already been bandaged up.

I kept asking where the helicopter was, and they kept telling me, "Ten minutes, it's coming in ten minutes, we just talked to them."

But lying on the ground, time wasn't my friend, and I kept saying, "Man, where's the helicopter?" They'd say ten minutes, and I'd respond, "You just told me ten minutes."

It ended up being an hour from the time I got hurt to the time the helicopter could get in to get me. But the boys took care of me. Rick and Thys cleared an area for the helicopter to land, and a little while before I was choppered out, the medic gave me a fentanyl lollipop to try to cut down my pain. I was supposed to suck on it, but I was hurting pretty bad, so I didn't listen to him. I chewed it, the whole thing. I had snapped my leg in half, torn my femoral artery, but the heat from the blast had cauterized it, and those burns were the most painful out of everything.

They loaded me onto the Black Hawk and flew me to Role 3, the U.S. hospital at Kandahar Airfield. By the time I arrived, I'd had my lollipop and was feeling pretty good. They opened the doors, and I remember there were all these people standing there waiting to roll me right into emergency surgery. There were a couple of guys that I recognized, and I said, "Oh my god, there's a welcoming committee! What's going on?" And they all thought, *Holy Jesus, this guy is laughing and he just blew his leg off.*

A lot of people began doing a lot of things all at once. I got IVs in both arms and there were tubes everywhere. I said to the doc, "I know my foot's gone, just save my knee."

When I woke up, I had tubes in both arms and nerve blocks out of both sides of my legs. They hadn't closed up my leg, and on the end was a wound vac, which looks like a sponge, but acts like a little vacuum and sucks out infection and dirt. The doctor told me that he couldn't save my knee, that my leg had bled out. The tourniquet had stopped blood from getting to it, but had also kept me alive. Life before limb, as they say.

Some guys came to see me later on, not from my section because they were still out in the field. I remember Rob O'Keefe asking how I was doing.

"It's a little bit of a rough day," I said. "I'm doing all right except for this little fella." And I wiggled what was left of my leg under the covers.

Everyone asked what they could do for me, and I said that all I wanted was a Tim Hortons coffee, a Timmy's. They went out, but Tim's ended up being closed that day, so they brought me something from Green Beans, I think.

I was conscious, and I was told I had to call home and let my family know I was all right. It would be better coming from me than the doctors.

I called my brother, and it was three days after his birthday, so when I got him on the line, I said, "Happy birthday. I'm sorry I missed it."

"It's good to hear from you," he replied. "What's on the go?"

"Oh, I had a bad day." It was hard to say the words.

"What do you mean?"

"I stepped on an IED this morning and I just lost my leg."

He paused. "Man, that's not funny. Don't joke around about that shit."

"I'm not joking. I'm lying in a hospital bed right now."

"You're wishing me a happy birthday and you're lying there without a leg?"

"Uh-huh." Despite everything I had been through in the last twelve hours, talking to my family was the hardest thing. I couldn't help but feel like I had let them down.

After a day or two, they flew me to Bagram, the northern air force base in Afghanistan, where I had another surgery, then from there I went to Germany on a big Airbus full of ISAF. Just a bunch of broken people who had been shot or blown up. We were on stretchers stacked three high on each side of the plane. I was on the top because I needed to have my head elevated, and I remember we were joking around with one another as much as we could. Some of the injuries were worse than others, so a couple of guys were telling the others to suck it up.

When we landed in Germany, they opened the big cargo door on the plane, and the first thing I smelled were the trees. That will stick with me forever, just being able to smell the trees.

The medical team had a hard time stabilizing me, and they weren't sure if I was going to make it home, so they flew my family out to see me. I didn't know that they were coming until they were there in my hospital room. That was even more difficult, because I didn't want them to see me the way I was, lying in a bed full of tubes.

I was still in Germany when I heard that Rick Cicero, the dog handler who had helped save me, was there too. He had gotten blown up just four days after me. Another IED. I was getting blood, so I couldn't go see him, but I wrote a letter for his son who was overseas at the time and coming to see Rick. I have no idea what I wrote, but I remember trying to explain how awesome his dad was and how he'd helped me.

After five or six days, I flew home with a flight surgeon on one of the government jets and started my rehab at the Ottawa Rehab Centre. There were a few guys and a girl who had arrived in rehab before me, so I had people to hang out with, to talk to and to try to figure out where we were going to go from there. The Ottawa Rehab Centre was amazing, and my doctor and physios were so supportive. I have them on Facebook and we chat it up still sometimes.

Rehab was challenging. I went from fighting in a war to being in a wheelchair. I had just turned twenty-five when I started rehab, and I was learning how to walk again. Learning how to put a leg on, to even say "put a leg on," was something new.

I remember the first day they fit me with a prosthetic. I was standing there in between bars with people watching me trying to learn how to walk, and I got extremely mad. I was so angry that day. Somebody had taken so much from me; they had taken from me the ability to even stand and walk.

Recovery for me was a mental game. Our bodies always adjust to the best of their abilities, but being positive, putting things into perspective—which is a whole lot easier to say than do—is the key to overcoming. I knew if I could think that way, then my body would follow.

I kept my leg on for fifteen, twenty minutes at a time, until it began to hurt, then went back to my wheelchair or my crutches. Every day, I did my exercises and kept my leg on longer and longer. I started walking for an hour with a cane, then walking twenty minutes without a cane. I learned how to walk up and down hills, stairs, curbs, everything you don't think about on a regular basis. Everything took longer than I wanted it to, but what helped the most was making myself talk about the day I lost my leg. At first, it was extremely hard, then it got easier and easier. I was able to talk about it, think about it, and process it.

I connected with Soldier On right away, and I believe they are part of the reason I recovered so quickly. A lot of people who are suffering like to hide away in their homes, but Soldier On is all about bringing people together and bringing them back to active lifestyles. When Greg Lagacé and his team came into the rehab centre, they said to me, "Hey, we're going skiing. Do you want to come?"

I was shocked. "Skiing? I'm just learning how to walk!"

But they were so confident. We talked to the prosthetic people there, and they said, "We can help you out. You can ski."

They ended up building me a prosthetic for snowboarding. I had never snowboarded before, so I had nothing to base it on. I was learning something new. But I got out and spent a week on the hills, six to seven months after I'd lost my leg.

I lost my leg on July 31, 2010, and in September they started building me a prosthetic, and within a few months I was walking, then running. By January, I was out of rehab and back at work half days. That was the thing I needed the most—to go back to something that was normal. I had a lot of support from the regiment and would spend half the day in rehab on base, swimming and walking and running, then the other half I would spend at work, trying to get some normality back in my life.

I'm stubborn. I'm still a combat engineer. I'm still 100 percent a soldier. In 2015 I was cleared for active duty. It was a long road to get there.

By 2012, I was teaching at the Canadian Forces School of Military Engineering in Gagetown. That's when I met my wife. She supports me no matter what. On my rough days, she's there to help me and sometimes give me that little kick that I need. She's my best friend and the love of my life. I don't know where I'd be without her.

In 2016, I applied to compete in the Invictus Games and was selected to join Team Canada. Because I was still an active service member, I needed to get permission from my chain of command to go. They were extremely supportive of my competing, so I went and represented Canada and the Engineer Corps. I rowed and attempted shot put, but didn't go very far. But I did well in max bench power lifting.

I just missed out on the bronze medal and ended up finishing fifth. This year I've been asked to be a mentor for the lifting team, so I'll be a competitor and a mentor. It's going to be good to have the games on Canadian soil in 2017. I've been working hard on my bench, so hopefully this year I'll be standing on a podium.

Invictus is an amazing experience because of the international scale—fifteen countries means that the level of competition is very high. But on the other hand, everyone has been beaten up or broken in some way, so even though we are competing against one another, we talk and joke with one another. Everybody there has gone through adversity and that is something we all respect, no matter what country.

My opinion of the Canadian Forces hasn't changed despite my injury. We are here to help people who can't help themselves. If I can pull an IED out of the ground, that's one less kid that might step on it and get killed.

Master Corporal Mark Hoogendoorn was born in Grimsby, Ontario, and joined the army in 2007 as a combat engineer. In April 2010, he deployed to Afghanistan with 1 RCR Battlegroup. He competed in the Invictus Games in Orlando, Florida, in 2016 and is slated to compete again in 2017. Mark lives with his wife and son in Fredericton, New Brunswick.

A normal day out in the desert.

Taking a break with Thys and Andrew while out on patrol.

My wife and me at our wedding with our son. This was one of the happiest days of my life.

I learned to snowboard less than a year after my accident. Now it's one of my favourite hobbies.

Looking out over the Atlantic Ocean from the shores of Prince Edward Island.

ACKNOWLEDGEMENTS

Jody Mitic: There are so many I'd like to thank for helping make this book a reality. First and foremost, I want to thank my fellow comrades in arms whose stories are printed on these pages. Thank you for being so generous with your time and sharing your experiences with me. And thank you to those who encouraged others to share.

To all my brothers and sisters in the Canadian Armed Forces and the veterans of Canada's military operations—you are the heroes and your lives inspire me every day. May we always support you.

To my agent, Brian Wood, thank you for your continued support.

To Luke, thanks—you know why!

To Kevin Hanson and Nita Pronovost, thank you for your vision for this book. To Sarah St. Pierre, big thank-you for helping me bring these people and their stories together. Thanks to Siobhan Doody for her tireless transcribing and to Jordyn Martinez for her enthusiastic recommendations, and to Patricia Ocampo and Alexandra Boelsterli for your help behind the scenes. Thanks also to my publicist, Rita Silva, for her support on and off the road.

I owe so much to my family—Mom, Dad, Katie, and Cory. Thank you for putting up with me and my schedule, and for supporting me in everything I do. A big thank-you to my girls, Alannah, Aylah, and Kierah, for bringing so much joy into my life.

Stuart Crawford: Thanks to the late Paul Davoud and my late brother Don for being with me in Europe during those few days in April 1945. Thanks to my wife, Mary, for her help in writing this story.

J. W. (Bill) Fitsell: Thanks to Stuart Crawford for getting me involved in this project. Thanks to Simon & Schuster Canada for the opportunity to tell my story.

Michael Czuboka: As a veteran who served with 2nd Battalion, PPCLI in Korea in what has often been called "Canada's forgotten war," I am very grateful for the editor's interest in the lives of past and present members of the Canadian Armed Forces.

Leonard Wells: I'd like to thank all who served for Canada.

Mort Lightstone: I acknowledge United States Air Force Colonel Glenn Jones, who served his country and the free world for more than thirty years diligently and without compromise.

Ron Cleroux: I'd like to acknowledge The Committee: Tonto, Devin, John, Adam, Grabbers, and my ever-loving wife, Nickie (Bird), who puts up with me and The Committee.

Trevor Jain: My story is dedicated to the reserve soldiers of Canada, twice the citizens called upon to leave their jobs and families to serve in time of need.

Kelly S. Thompson: I'm grateful to the Forces, which has not only shaped the moral framework of four generations of my family—and my husband and me too—but also provided me with stories and friendships to last ten books. And to Joe, for carrying me for three kilometres, for smiling the whole damn time, and, ten years later, for becoming my husband.

William Munden: I am grateful to Simon & Schuster for giving me the opportunity to relate the story of the "Buffalo Nine" and to remind Canadians that the anniversary of the tragedy, August 9, has been set aside as National Peacekeepers' Day.

Ron Rivers: The military was a whole new thing for me. I didn't understand much at the young age of eighteen when I enlisted, and I wouldn't have completed what was involved without the help of my fellow soldiers. Thank you to my comrades for your friendship and support, and for showing me how to pay it forward. I will never forget my brothers.

Tim Isberg: To my fellow military observers and the many civilian friends in the humanitarian community who served tirelessly amidst the chaos of Rwanda 1994–95, know that you made a difference, not the very least to me.

Trevor Smith: I'd like to thank all my instructors and section commanders from basic up to my retirement. Without their mentoring I wouldn't have made it to where I am today. Most of all I'd like to thank my dad, Bruce, for instilling discipline and a sense of pride in myself that served me well through my career and continues today in my retirement. You are dearly missed. *Pro Patria* and *Arte et Marte!*

Lisa Ouellette: I would like to thank my wife, Lisa Michaud. She has been with me through thick and thin. She is my best friend, my person, my rock! *Ch'teume!* I would love to thank my mother, Margot Ouellette; she has always been there when I needed her. She has taken the role of my mother and my father after my dad passed. Her positivity and understanding helped me become a better person. I love you! And I would like to thank my big brother David Ouellette. He has been a father figure to me after the passing of my dad; he is a warm-hearted person. Thank you for making me the godmother of your daughter Emma. I love you! *Va po trop vite.*

Donald Hookey: I would like to thank my family for all their support not only for the story but for all the years I served in the CAF.

Bruno Guévremont: I would like to thank my friends and family for their incredible support during my military career. But I would especially like to thank my C-IED Team for all coming back home in one piece.

Andy Gill: I would like to thank my mom, dad, wife, and daughter.

David Quick: I would only like to thank my two daughters, Willow and Shaeffer, for remaining my strength and my motivation and for reminding me that there is perfection in life. I am a better man because of you two ladies. I would do it all over again to have you in my life. Thank you for letting me be your daddy. I have never been happier.

D. Brett Irwin: To the soldiers of 7 Platoon Oscar Company Task Force 1-10. *Pro Patria.*

Justin Bronzan: I am truly humbled by this book, as well as by the opportunities and eye-opening experiences of a lifetime.

Mark Hoogendoorn: To everyone who kept me alive. Thank you.

PHOTO CREDITS

117 Hangar B, Suite B, and Trevor with Lee Fraser: Courtesy of Trevor Jain.

133 Joe and Kelly and Kelly in her kit: Courtesy of Kelly Thompson.

149 Portrait: Courtesy of Nancy Munden.

149 Labrador helicopter: Courtesy of William Munden.

150 Logbook and Buffalo Nine ceremony: Courtesy of William Munden.

151 Logbook and Hercules 307: Courtesy of William Munden.

161 Basic training group, graduation photo, and Suffield training: Courtesy of Ron Rivers.

176 Portrait and August 15 diary entry: Courtesy of Tim Isberg.

177 January 5 and April 6 diary entries: Courtesy of Tim Isberg.

192 In basic training: Courtesy of Trevor Smith.

192 Trevor with his uncle, Jim: Courtesy of Shelley Smith.

192 Trevor at the one-hundredth anniversary ceremony: Courtesy of the *Eganville Leader*.

203 Suiting up in Strensall and the Strensall facility: Courtesy of Lisa Ouellette.

204 Sierra Leone checkpoint and Lisa in Sierra Leone: Courtesy of Lisa Ouellette.

217 In the HLVW: Courtesy of Donald Hookey.

217 Readying the mortars: Courtesy of U.S. Staff Sergeant Ron Busbin.

229 Timer, booby-trapped wire, and bomb suit: Courtesy of Master Warrant Officer Terry Garand.

239 Living quarters: Courtesy of Andy Gill.

239 Keeping watch: Courtesy of Corporal Cam Smith.

239 With the ANP: Courtesy of Corporal J. Taylor.

253 Operation Dragon Strike: Courtesy of David Quick.

253 With Prince Phillip: Courtesy of the Department of National Defence.

266 Brett in Petawawa: Courtesy of Dave Irwin.

266 After first gunfight: Courtesy of Brett Irwin.

267 At COP Panjshir and C-6 GPM: Courtesy of Brett Irwin.

280 Sandstorm: Courtesy of Brett Irwin.

281 With Brett and coming back from patrol: Courtesy of Brett Irwin.

294 In the desert and taking a break: Courtesy of Mark Hoogendoorn.

295 Wedding photo: Courtesy of Adventure Photos.

295 Snowboarding and at PEI: Courtesy of Mark Hoogendoorn.

ABOUT THE EDITOR

Jody Mitic is a twenty-year Canadian Armed Forces veteran and sniper team leader. A sought-after motivational speaker, he is a respected advocate for wounded veterans, people with disabilities, and amputees. His memoir, *Unflinching: The Making of a Canadian Sniper,* is a perennial bestseller. He founded the Never Quit Foundation and currently sits on the board of directors of Won with One, an organization devoted to helping physically challenged athletes realize their dreams. He currently serves on the Ottawa City Council.

🐦 @JODYMITIC